BYRD

This is reputed to be the only existing portrait of Byrd, but its authenticity is unsupported by better evidence than that it was engraved by Vandergucht, together with a similar portrait of Tallis, for a *History of Music* which was projected in the eighteenth century by Nicolo Haym but did not appear. Haym came to England in 1704 and at one time wrote librettos for Handel. He became a collector of pictures from two of which he probably copied the heads of Tallis and Byrd. Hawkins relates that he published the prospectus of his proposed *History of Music* in 1729, but he died soon after.

(Royal College of Music)

[*front*

WILLIAM BYRD

BY

FRANK HOWES

Author of *The Borderland of Music and Psychology*

GREENWOOD PRESS, PUBLISHERS
WESTPORT, CONNECTICUT

Library of Congress Cataloging in Publication Data

Howes, Frank Stewart, 1891-
    William Byrd.

    Reprint of the 1928 ed. published by K. Paul,
Trench, Trubner, London, issued in series:
Masters of music.
    Includes index.
    1. Byrd, William, 1542 or 3-1623.   2.   Composers
--England--Biography.
ML410.B996H7   1978   780'.92'4   [B]   77-27081
ISBN 0-313-20182-X

Reprinted with the permission of Routledge and Kegan Paul, Ltd.

Reprinted in 1978 by Greenwood Press, Inc.,
51 Riverside Avenue
Westport, CT. 06880

Printed in the United States of America

10 9 8 7 6 5 4 3 2 1

CONTENTS

LIST OF ILLUSTRATIONS

PREFACE

THIS study of William Byrd does not profess to be *the* book which someone must write some day when all the composer's music is available to all musicians. But its author hopes that it may be useful as the first attempt to paint a portrait of the man. There is a view widely held that the lives of composers and their music are two entirely different things and that it is a source of confusion and error to interpret either in terms of the other. This view I believe to be wrong psychologically. Everyone of us has one mind, which can do many different kinds of work but which is not a bundle of faculties. Except in pathological cases we must assume the unity of personality, and my view of Byrd as a man I derive both from his anthems and from his lawsuits—both were products of the same mind. Of his compositions which are the chief source of our knowledge of that mind, not all are published even yet ; but thanks to the devoted labours of Dr E. H. Fellowes and others, more than enough are already available in modern reprints for us to form an estimate of the composer which cannot be substantially changed by subsequent additions to our present rich store. The criticism in this book is based on music which anyone can now obtain, I had almost said from any music shop, but that is an exaggeration, since

copies of Breitkopf and Haertel's edition of the
Fitzwilliam Virginal Book are now hard to come
by. I was fortunate enough however to have
access to the copy in the library of the Oxford
University Musical Club. I was also fortunate
in obtaining from Mr. W. Barclay Squire, most
generous of scholars, in the year before he died,
the loan of his MS. score of the *Gradualia* which
were not published at the time when I made my
study of Byrd's Latin Church music, but which
have recently appeared in Volume VII of the
Carnegie series of Tudor Church Music. The
greatest gaps in our knowledge of Byrd's music
occur in the *Cantiones Sacrae* of 1575 and 1591,
of which few have so far been scored and published
in modern editions. But apart from these,
a good library or a long purse will produce
modern printed copies of most of Byrd's important compositions. I have added an appendix,
which, though undoubtedly incomplete, will
supply information about the prices and publishers of modern editions of Byrd's many and
varied works.

Anyone who investigates the music of the
Elizabethan period finds himself immediately
indebted to at least three men : to Sir Richard
Terry, who by performance of the music stimulated interest in its revival and who has edited
some of Byrd's work ; to the late Mr. Barclay
Squire, for his researches both biographical and
musical and for his editorial work in conjunction

with Mr. J. A. Fuller-Maitland on the *Fitzwilliam Virginal Book*; and most of all to Dr. E. H. Fellowes, for the text of the actual music which he has provided in reliable and scholarly editions. Dr. Fellowes has put musicians still further in his debt by the concise guides he has written to Byrd's career and music in his *English Madrigal Composers*, in his monograph *William Byrd* published for the tercentenary in 1923 and in various prefaces. In addition to these authorities, I have also consulted the *Oxford History of Music*, Dr. Ernest Walker's *History of Music in England*, various writings of Mr. H. B. Collins, Dr. Grattan Flood, Dr. Naylor, and Mr. Van Den Borren.

I wish also to express my gratitude to Mr. Noel Ponsonby, of Christ Church, Oxford, for reading my MS, and to Mrs. Thomas Wood for reading my proofs and making the index; to Mr. J. B. Trend for a valuable suggestion and the loan of Cabezon's music; to Canon F. W. Galpin for permission to quote from his *Old English Instruments of Music*, to the Rev. E. H. L. Reeve for permission to quote from his history of the parish of Stondon Massie; to Mr. Fuller-Maitland for permission to quote from the introduction to the published edition of *The Fitzwilliam Virginal Book*; to Mr. C. W. Beaumont and Miss Hilda Andrews for permission to make certain quotations from their works; to the late Mr. Barclay Squire and the editor of the third edition of Grove's *Dictionary of Music and Musicians* for allowing me to consult the article on Byrd before it was published; to Mr. Gerald Cooper for permitting me to consult his card-index of Byrd's virginal compositions; to the Royal College of Music for the reproduction of Byrd's portrait. My gratitude to Mr. H. C. Colles for help in this as in many other undertakings I shall try to express by inscribing this work to him in acknowledgment of a chronic debt, which has a happy way of eluding settlement.

This book was originally designed as one of a series, not of great musicians, but of great men of all kinds. This fact determined the form of the book and led me to include explanations of technical terms which musical readers may resent as an affront to their intelligence. When the book outgrew its original design I thought well to retain these footnotes and the translations of all Latin words and sentences, so that if it fell into the hands of the general reader it might be reasonably intelligible to him. Personal explanations are to be avoided if possible, but I think I had better say in view of the religious issues involved in Byrd's career, and to avoid possible misapprehension of what I have written in the last chapter, that I am not and never have been a full member of any Christian communion.

FRANK HOWES.

December, 1927.

WILLIAM BYRD

CHAPTER I

THE MODERN APPROACH

IN the year 1842, three hundred years (all but one) after the composer's birth, the Musical Antiquarian Society of London brought out an edition of some of the works of William Byrd. They entrusted the task of selecting and editing the *Cantiones Sacræ* (a collection of motets or anthems), to a certain William Horsley. This gentleman had spent his life in the practice of music and had reached the age of sixty-eight when he undertook this task; his judgment may therefore be considered fully ripe. Furthermore he held the degree of Bachelor of Music in the University of Oxford, and so knew what he was talking about. His editorial preface begins with a sinister-sounding appeal to Truth. 'Truth, and truth alone, should be the Critic's great object, as well as of the Historian.' When people begin to talk like this they usually intend to say something unpleasant, else why make all the fuss about telling the truth like an honest man ? After several paragraphs of excellent moral principles in which he puts aside the bias of petty resentment, petty interest, pride and prejudice he begins to reveal the horrid truth.

'These observations I have thought necessary', he writes, 'because a minute examination has led me to form a very different opinion of the *Cantiones Sacræ* to that which I formerly entertained. Judging from a few favourable specimens, and trusting, as I am bound to confess, too much to the applause which has been lavished on them for more than two centuries, I had formed notions of their excellence which exist in my mind no longer. It would be the height of folly and injustice to apply many of our modern rules of Composition to the Works of the Fathers of English ecclesiastical Music. But it must be remembered that these works have been held up to us, by poets and historians, as being almost models of perfection.'

He then proceeds to make his criticisms and substantiate them with examples of technical errors, and draws this final conclusion:

'That the work is curious, and worthy of being reprinted by the Musical Antiquarian Society may be readily admitted. We must however bear in mind that the examples it furnishes are of a School long since passed away, and that (like other music of the time) it contains principles of composition no longer received.'

In the year 1925 a writer in *The Musical Times*[1] in complaining of the artificiality of much

[1] *Musical Times*, January, 1925, p. 22.

contemporary music, gives as an example of the affectations of composers the overdoing of 'the fashionable Byrdisms'. What was out of date in 1842 has become fashionable in 1925! 'Principles of composition no longer received' have become the very latest thing! But in truth, though the too-sedulous imitation of some of Byrd's technical methods may be tiresome, there has been in the last quarter of a century a complete change of attitude towards the great school of English composers of the Elizabethan period, of whom Byrd was the pioneer, the father, and on any comprehensive reckoning the greatest.

This change is not something that just happened of its own accord here in England. It is part of a very much wider tendency. We regard, quite rightly, the death of Queen Victoria as marking a turning point in our attitude to almost every department of life. The turning process was not completed until the European War gave it a sharp wrench farther into the new direction. Neither did Victorianism die suddenly—it survives still, and the pioneers of all that we roughly call 'modern tendencies' in politics, in social custom, in religion, and in art were most of them busy before 1900 dawned. But on any broad view of recent history it is undeniable that a great change has come over society in the first quarter of the twentieth century, a change which in most ways is a reaction from Victorian standards and ideals.

One sees it in the arts uncomplicated by factors like the development of scientific invention which has affected the social sciences. Present taste is all in the direction of simplicity, even in women's clothes; in decoration plain styles and pure if vivid colours prevail; plain speaking and writing are required by a generation that has known war; in architecture the austerity of the Bush building in Aldwych, London, is preferred to the encrustations of ornament which were formerly mistaken for architectural beauty. Indeed ornamentation is the centre of the whole change. Nowadays if for any reason a rich effect is desired, no architect attempts to get it by dabbing on to his structures irrelevant scrolls and bosses and humps; festoons are out of favour and for every excrescence there must be some logical justification in the ground plan of the whole design. The opposite principle is seen at its English high-water-mark in the Albert Memorial, where every kind of stone that was ever quarried is pitched together, sometimes as itself, sometimes disguised as wood or metal; where plain granite columns are surmounted by prickly ornaments, and a marble frieze is offset by little patches of gold leaf. Not that ornamentation need be as bad as this—the baroque buildings of southern Europe carry off this sort of thing with more dash than the stolid Englishman could master. But even when it is well done, we do not like it now. We are in the mood for the unadorned, for strong lines, for

4

austerity.   The music of Byrd has these characteristics which have made this generation of musicians
turn to him.

If we confine our attention to the single art of
music but go out into the wider field of European
composition, we find the same tendencies showing
themselves.   Richard Strauss is still writing music
of the same kind which just before the War was
regarded as the last word in advanced cacophony.
For sheer cacophony we can do better than that
nowadays, and the amusing thing is that he is
now too rich for our taste.   He is seen to be
essentially Victorian in style.   His method is to
add sound to sound, colour to colour, instrument
to instrument, and his magnificence is due to the
fact that he can make an adequate framework
upon which to weave elaborate designs with the
infinite ornaments of the modern orchestra.   The
' new ', i.e. the twentieth-century, music has
turned its ears in another direction ; it has turned
to the old scales of the Middle Ages and sought
to develop something new from them, it has
sought to make strong rather than sweet sounds,
and sometimes its sounds are very strong ; it has
(in England at any rate) looked for inspiration to
the simplicity of folk-song.   Modern European
music has one or other of two qualities and neither
is the lusciousness of Strauss.   Much of it is
stark, the rest is vague and atmospheric, like shapes
seen through a softening mist.   The modern
musician in fact has reacted in two opposite

5

directions from the sentiment, the romance and the richness of the nineteenth century which culminated in Wagner. It seems fairly safe to say that he has not yet attained to a greatness comparable to that of the giants of the last century; he may or may not do. That is neither here nor there; what is important is that his endeavours are now turned not to climbing the same range of hills but to beginning the ascent of the next range, which is of radically different formation. One consequence of this reaction, at first sight curious but soon seen to be natural, is the renewed enthusiasm for the early composers from Bach backwards. The revival of interest in our Elizabethans is one, but only one, manifestation of a taste that can bear nothing written between 1790 and 1900.

These hundred and ten years hang together as an epoch in musical history. In it, beside the widening of the main stream, developments took place in a number of loops and side channels—the piano was perfected and influenced the style of musical composition, the song was given a new life of its own by Schubert, dramatic and descriptive music became at once more vivid and more serious under the influence of Berlioz and Wagner. And so one could go on setting one distinguished name after another against great achievements in the development of music. But the main problem of all musicians in this period was to exploit to the

6

full all the possibilities of instrumental music. Vocal and operatic music soon absorbed the new possibilities discovered by the instruments, but the main line of advance lay in the evolution of satisfactory form, of musical architecture and of a tremendously expressive harmony. This is not to suggest that form comes before 'content' in music. All this time the range of human experience expressible in music was rapidly growing, and composers in seeking to give utterance to their new visions hewed out for themselves the new technical means required to express them. But the technical aspect, as we have already seen in the Albert Memorial, reflects always an inner working of the spirit, and in this case the technical side can be examined under the microscope more easily than the spirit which uses it as a vehicle. Haydn had lain down the foundations of the symphony, on which Mozart, Beethoven, and all the later symphonists down to Brahms have built, and the essential principle of his architecture which gives unity to a piece of instrumental music is the disposition of themes in certain key-relationships. The working out of key-relationships has given rise to modern harmony which reached its furthest point in Wagner. There was for the moment no further progress to be made in that direction. The interest of composers therefore began to look once more in a direction which 150 years previously had seemed to have reached a final point of development in

7

Bach, i.e., towards counterpoint. The difference
between these two aspects of music, the harmonic
and the contrapuntal, must be made quite clear.
The distinction must be clear, yet there is no
sharp line of demarcation between harmony and
counterpoint. As the early writers of counterpoint soon found, you cannot combine melodies
without becoming immediately aware that certain
combinations of sound are intolerable to the
human ear, i.e., that while each melody may be
quite satisfactory in itself, it jostles its neighbour
with a sharp clash at certain points ; these clashes
are rejected by the ear for harmonic reasons.
Contrariwise when a musician tries to 'harmonize'
a tune, i.e. combine other sounds with the notes
of the main tune so as to form an accompaniment
for it, he may find that certain combinations of
notes sounded simultaneously and pleasing enough,
cannot be utilized because they are difficult to
approach from the previous notes of the several
parts (what a musician calls difficult intervals).
In this case his harmony is obstructed for contrapuntal reasons. Harmony and counterpoint,
then, are two ways of looking at the same thing,
viz. progressions of sounds. Harmony is usually
described as the vertical way, counterpoint as
the horizontal. It is impossible to have one
without the other, because all music except a
single melody has two dimensions—forward
motion and simultaneity. A simple experiment
will make clear the root difference between these

two aspects of music.   If you sing, or play on the
piano

you have a tune, of an elementary character, but
still a tune which moves forward.   But if you put
down the keys

you produce a completely different mental effect.
Somehow the three notes lose part of their
identity and fuse in some mysterious way into a
kind of smooth single sound, not three but one.
This is harmony.   No. 1 is not yet counterpoint
which requires at least two tunes to be going at
once, but it has the horizontal movement which
counterpoint requires.   At present it is only a
tune. And from the dawn of time until the early
Middle Ages Europeans asked for nothing more
from their music than simple tunes, and a great
part of humanity is still content with very little
more.   This little more is the drone.
The effect of sounding a drone bass underneath
a tune is one of contrast.   The movement of the
tune is heightened by being compared with the
stationary bass, which acts as a kind of lever and
lends wings to the tune.   This soaring effect is
characteristic of counterpoint.   The drone bass

curiously enough does not blend harmonically with the notes above it, and when it is used in harmonic passages (where it is technically called a 'pedal' because it is a characteristic effect of the pedal department of the organ) it almost always creates the effect, not of being safely anchored, but of dragging at the anchor with ever-increasing power.

As a matter of historical development, in the early mediæval Church, which was the cradle of all the music we know to-day except folk-song, singing in parts arose out of the natural fact that men cannot all sing comfortably at the same pitch, and that boys and women sing an octave higher than the men. What happened therefore was that congregations sang the same plain-song at different pitches, the four parts running strictly parallel to each other at the interval of a fourth and a fifth, like this :

(Quoted by Wooldridge, *Oxford History of Music*, Vol. I, p. 51, from *Musica Enchiriadis*, a treatise of the tenth century.)

This parallelism (technically called ' Organum ')
produces a crude kind of harmony, and marks a
stage in the development of counterpoint in that
the singers would feel that their melodies had a
measure of independence. In course of time it
was superseded, not to be employed again until
the twentieth century, when Debussy, Vaughan
Williams (in the G minor Mass) and others took
up parallel motion once more and used this
ancient device to extend their modern idiom.
Developments in this plural melody took place in
the eleventh century: oblique motion, in which
the lowest voice sometimes had to stand still on
the lowest note of the organs of the day while the
plain song moved above it, and finally contrary
motion, in which the two voices, the principal
and the organal, move in opposite directions.
This was counterpoint, point against point, i.e.
note against note.

A further measure of independence is necessary
to each part before the characteristic contrapuntal
effect is to prevail over the harmonic. The strict
note-against-note principle has to give way to
greater variety of rhythm : a bass may have to
sing two or three shorter notes while the tenor is
singing one long note, and each part has to obtain
freedom to employ notes of different time-values.
In other words, freedom of rhythm becomes
necessary as well as freedom of melodic shape.
When this has been obtained the voices will also
claim for themselves the right to enter separately

and to pursue their own courses, subject only to the limitations of fitting in with the general conception of the whole composition and of making a pleasing sound.

Musical composition had reached this point of development in England by about 1230, the approximate date of the famous round *Sumer is icumen in*. This is a song with a fresh lilting melody so constructed that it may be sung by four voices, each of which enters four bars after the last and sings the same tune.[1] Since therefore it is essentially a weaving together of melodies, its musical interest is contrapuntal. It has however a simple recurring bass in two parts to the words *Sing, cuccu, nu, sing cuccu*, which determines its very simple harmonic scheme. Regarded merely as harmony, however, it would be intolerably tedious, consisting as it does of ceaseless repetition of the same progression of four chords, but as in any other good contrapuntal work the harmonies thus made are in themselves smooth and satisfying to the ear. The music of the sixteenth century and of William Byrd in particular is contrapuntal in the same sort of way; the interest lies in the weaving of the parts rather than in the progression of blocks of sound, though the parts must flow forward in such a way as not to outrage the ear

---

[1] This musical device is technically called a canon. When, as in this case, the first voice having come to the end of the tune may begin it again and still combine with the parts still going on, the composition is called a round.

at any point by the simultaneous occurrence of two or more incompatible sounds.

It has been necessary to go into the question of harmony and counterpoint at some length, because in approaching the vocal music of the Elizabethan period the listener may save himself disappointment if he knows what to listen for and what not to expect. For the modern ear has accustomed itself to a different treatment of melodies. About the year 1600 in Italy a movement began in revolt against the contrapuntal methods of composition which then held the field. At its best (as in the works of Palestrina) that style of writing produced works of severe and ethereal beauty, at its worst it lent itself to an undue exploitation of mere ingenuity which ended in an artistic desert. The reformers wished something different from both. They wished music to portray with greater vividness a greater range of emotion, including passions that were neither severe nor ethereal. They therefore turned to melody unfettered by the requirements of combination with other melodies. Get first the tune which will say with the maximum of force what you desire to express and subordinate everything else to enhancing its effect ; this was their aim. Thus began a movement which has proved very fertile to music, for while it has led to the supremacy of a single melody not only in vocal music but in the masterpieces of the great symphonists, it has also led to the development of harmony through the last 300 years which has already been mentioned. Tune and harmony, then, are what the ordinary musical person first looks for. Hearing a hymn sung, for example, the listener will only be aware of the tune and of a vague pleasant noise supporting it. Even in *Glory to thee, my God, this night* to Tallis' canon, he will probably not be aware that the tune appears in the tenor as well as the treble. It is quite possible that such a person hearing a madrigal for the first time (or even Bach for that matter) will be aware of a quarrelsome confusion rather than anything else, especially if he is obliged to approach this music through the gramophone. But if he complains that there is no tune for him to get hold of he is making a wrong diagnosis : what he means is that there are too many tunes.

Another adjustment of mind and ear which he must make is to the apparently unexciting character of all this early music, both vocal and instrumental. Not only popular music with its battery of jazz instruments but every kind of music written since the invention of the piano, not excluding voices or the string quartet, has grown more forceful in expression. In Byrd's day all music was vocal in style ; instrumental music was feeling after its independence but it had not at that time worked out for itself either a style or a self-sufficient formal structure. Vocal music is strongly affected in both these respects by the words that are to be sung, which impose their own rhythm upon it. The rhythm of Elizabethan music requires separate discussion ; its foundation is not the strong regularly recurring accent which is the characteristic of all music since the late seventeenth century. Instrumental music, in seeking a structure that would give unity and order to what would otherwise appear like a vague flow of sound, turned from poetry to the dance, where a strong regular accent is a physical necessity. This kind of rhythm, once found, proved to be capable of very rich development and, what is more, a most flexible means of expressing emotion. Voices, which are wind instruments and so produce a more or less continuous flow of sound, are not capable of emphasizing this regular accentuation without sounding ridiculous. Indeed the art of poetry on its technical side consists in clothing a rhythmic skeleton of regular accents with a succession of words whose natural speech accents run across and conceal the ding-dong metre of the verse. The dance, however, makes use of a rhythmic scheme in which weak accents group themselves round strong accents in regular recurring sequences. This rhythmic principle of construction had no sooner become well established than along came Beethoven, one of the most emotionally explosive persons who have ever expressed themselves in music, and worked the dynamic side of music for all it was worth, employing devices which have

15

since been worked for much more than they are worth by jazz bands. Beethoven was led into this kind of writing largely through the mere accident that the piano had been invented in time for him to write his sonatas for it instead of the old harpsichords, on which almost nothing could be done in the way of accentuation. The piano is an instrument of percussion ; the strings are hit with hammers, and the harder they are hit the louder the note and the stronger the accent that is produced ; moreover, the accents can be distributed at will. It is not to be supposed that in all music played and sung before this there was no feeling of regular rhythm, for the mind will supply accents to a series of sounds merely according to their position and duration ; but what Beethoven and his successors have done much more extensively than the earlier composers is to reinforce these natural accents with accents of stress, and it is largely this which has made modern music exciting. In listening to the music of the sixteenth century the listener has to shed the accumulated excitements of three centuries, and he will find in doing so an extraordinary sense of refreshment. Its peaceful intimacy will soothe him like a hot bath after a journey, its simplicity and austerity will invigorate him like a cold bath after a restless night.

CHAPTER II

MUSIC BEFORE ELIZABETH'S REIGN

SEEN in retrospect the whole Tudor period (which may be taken to include the reign of James I which came to an end in 1625) appears as an epoch of astonishing national vigour. The force of political circumstance certainly played a large part in moulding the eventful careers of Henry VIII and Elizabeth, and so far these monarchs were products of their age. But their own vigorous personalities no less certainly helped to shape the destinies of their country and their epoch. In either case it is plain that Henry VIII was a man of remarkable abilities. In his early days he was a good athelete, and to the end of his life was enthusiastic about every kind of intellectual pursuit. Among the accomplishments to which he owed some of his early popularity was a high degree of musical skill. An eye witness in describing his attractions, physical, linguistic, athletic and intellectual says that he ' plays well on the lute and harpsichord, sings from the book at sight, draws the bow, etc.'[1] Not only did he practice diligently, but he listened to a great deal of music. It is recorded for instance that he and his Court listened for four hours on end to the organ recitals of Dionysius Memo, the Venetian

[1] *Letters and Papers of Henry VIII*, ii, 395.

organist whom he had invited to England. Moreover he was a composer with a considerable number
of works to his credit; of these the best and
best-known is the vigorous song *Pastime with
Good Company* of which he wrote both words and
music.[1] Boyce in his collection of Cathedral
music, which he published in 1768, included an
anthem *O Lord, the Maker of all things,* which he
assigned to King Henry but is now known not
to be his work. If he never achieved a distinctive
style of his own, his devotion to and knowledge of
music, which he passed on to his children, were of
the greatest value to the art in England. For
the Tudor sovereigns were not nonentities, and
their enthusiasm influenced all the upper grades
of society, on whom devolved the cultivation of
the graces of civilization, much more strongly
than a tepid official support given by monarchs
whose personalities counted for less in the life
of their times. Henry set the fashion to be
musical, and for the next hundred years music
remained fashionable, to its great profit. Burney,
the eighteenth-century historian, quotes a list
of 'Musitions and Players' of the Household and
Chapel Royal of Edward VI, with their salaries.
From this it appears that the royal musical staff
consisted of sixteen trumpeters, two luters, two

---

[1] Lord Herbert of Cherbury said of him : 'He was (which one might
wonder in a king) a curious Musician, as two entire Masses composed by him
and often sung in his Chapel, did abundantly witness'; and Hollingshead
also testifies to his spending his leisure in 'plaieing at recorders, flute and
virginals, in setting of songs and making of ballads.'

harpers, two singers (beside the gentlemen of the Chapel Royal), one player of the rebecke (a fore-runner of the violin), six sackbuts, eight vyalls, one bagpiper, nine minstrelles, three dromslades (drummers), two players of the flute, three players on the virginals, six musitions straungers (of whom four were Venetians and brothers), eight players of interludes, and two makers of instruments (organ and regal[1]). Of these some would only have a ceremonial use and would have no direct effect upon the compositions of the period. A German traveller, for example, relates that during the setting of dinner at Elizabeth's court the hall rang with the sound of twelve trumpets and two drums. Even earlier in the century (1521) we read that :

> Certayne at eche course of service in the hall
> Trumpetts blewe up, Shalmes and Claryons
> Shewynge theyre melodye with toynes musycall.[2]

What these wind instruments played is not clear. Cornets and sackbuts (ancestors of the trombones) were used for reinforcing the choirs of the great cathedrals, but the shawms,[3] which were made

---

[1] The regal was a portable keyboard instrument like a harmonium.

[2] Quoted by Canon Galpin, *Old English Instruments of Music*, p. 275, from *The Life of S. Werberge*, printed by Pynson in 1521.

[3] The shawm is the forerunner of the oboe. Canon Galpin writes : ' The " Mynstrells " in the musical establishment of Henry VIII are identical with the " Shalmes " of his successor, and in the illustration of the banquets and jousts of the preceding century they are frequently depicted playing to the assembled guests. The increase in the size and numbers of the wind instruments during the XVI century added greatly to the importance of these bands.'

in several sizes, formed a wind-band of their own, and either with or without the help of other wind instruments were used by minstrels on festive occasions in pageants and dramatic entertainments ; and they were the instruments of the town ' waits '. To them therefore belongs the secular music of the period, which was still doubtless vocal in style but livelier than the ecclesiastical compositions. Instrumental compositions however did begin an independent life in the first half of the sixteenth century, and had grown up sufficiently by the time of Byrd to enable him and his contemporaries to take it out of the experimental stage and make music which is capable of giving us artistic pleasure to-day. The Elizabethan period did not, however, see the beginning of anything like our orchestral music. The Court had a large musical staff, as we have seen, and on occasion it turned out en masse, but the instrumentalists did not play all together. Thus at the production of *Gorbudoc* in 1561 the orchestra consisted of violins, cornets, flutes, hautboys and drums and fifes, but each section played separately.[1] This was in accordance

[1] The synopsis of this, the earliest Elizabethan tragedy of revenge, is of some interest to musicians.

' The order of the dumb-show before the first act, and the signification thereof. First the music of violins began to play, during which came in upon the stage five wild men clothed in leaves ; of whom the first bore on his neck a faggot of small sticks which they break ; music right through.

Act II.—First the music of cornets began to play, during which came upon the stage a King. King is poisoned and music plays right through action.

with the custom of the period to perform its music in ' consorts '. It was a ' whole consort ' when all the instruments were of one family— the viols, or the recorders, or the shawms, a ' broken consort ' if instruments of different families were combined. In an early fifteenth century manuscript a viol and a recorder are already to be seen playing in broken consort, and a hundred years later experiments are made with various collections of instruments. In 1599 Thomas Morley, one of Byrd's pupils, published a book called *The first Booke of Consort Lessons, made by divers exquisite Authors for six Instruments to play together, viz. the Treble Lute, the Pandora, the Citterne, the Base Violl, the Flute, and the Treble Violl.* And as late as 1672 Matthew Locke published *Compositions for Broken and Whole Consorts,* the whole consorts consisting of three viols, and the broken consort of the same instruments with the addition of the oboes and harpsichord. But there is not yet an orchestral *tutti* (all together), nor is there yet any notion of what we understand by scoring. Monteverde, for example, in his opera *Orfeo,* which appeared in 1609, prescribes a great number of instruments and at the head of each number he says which of

ACT III.—Music of flutes ; company of mourners.
ACT IV.—Music of hautboys. Three furies come from under the stage as if from out of Hell, clad in black garments sprinkled with blood and flames and their bodies girt with snakes—signifying murder.
ACT V.—Drums and flutes. Company of armed men, who discharge their pieces—signifying war.'

them are to play, but assigns no part to them. The individual players must have had parts to play from, but there could not have been the nice calculation of instrumental effects which is made possible by the precise modern method of assigning in the full score a line to each kind of instrument. There must have been much duplication, much variation in the choice of instruments available at different times and places, and much greater freedom of discretion left both to the orchestral players and to the conductor. In fact, we shall not have to look for anything remotely like orchestral music in the works of the great Elizabethans.

The ' whole consort ' however does lead directly to the string quartet, and in its development Byrd plays an important part. The consort of viols—violins though known in Elizabeth's day did not come into common use among musicians till the time of the Restoration—is the most important of these whole consorts, both because it at once showed in a marked degree its musical fitness to survive, and because ability to play on the viol was widely distributed among amateurs. When we come to consider secular vocal music we shall see that, though then as always composition is the life-work of the professionals, the less important though hardly less necessary work of performance was in Elizabethan days largely an amateur affair, and the vigorous musical life of the period is due to that fact. We shall find a good deal of evidence for the wide distribution and high standard of musical culture in the upper ranks of English society. People with any pretensions of breeding and education could play the viol, and every large household contained among its furniture a ' chest of viols '. Under these conditions it was natural that the delights of making concerted music should spread from voices to instruments. Domestic music parties looking for something to play together turned to the only music they knew that would suit their purpose— the madrigals, choosing perhaps for performance those they found difficult or impossible for some reason to sing—this one with the wide range beyond the compass of their alto, or that one with the peculiarly tiresome tenor part. Once the fascination of what we should now call string ensemble had been discovered, the demand for instrumental music increased ; and the introduction which Byrd wrote to his first volume of madrigals (1588) shows that by that time it was a recognized practice to use the madrigals either for singing, or for playing, or even for a half and half treatment, by which a missing voice might be ' filled in ' by a viol. In The Epistle to the Reader prefixed to *Psalms, Sonnets, and Songs* he writes :

' Benigne Reader, heere is offered vnto thy courteous acceptation, Musicke of sundrie sorts, and to content diuers humors. If thou bee disposed to praye, heere are *Psalmes*. If to bee merrie, heere are *Sonets*. If to lament for thy sins, heere are songs of sadness and *Pietie*. If thou delight in Musicke of great cōpasse, heere are diuers songs, which beeing originally made for Instruments to expresse the harmony, and one voyce to pronounce the dittie, are now framed in all parts for voyces to sing the same.' Further on in the same preface he has the phrase ' in the expressing of these songs, either by voyces or Instruments '. Nine years later Dowland, the composer of songs to the lute, published a volume of ' ayres ' which were ' so made that all the partes together, or either of them severally may be sung to the Lute, Orpherian or Viol de gambo '. In both of these publications we see the beginings of the idea of instrumental accompaniment to vocal music, though so far voices and instruments are regarded as alternative and loosely inter-changeable ways of performing the same music. By 1600, when Weelkes brought out his third set of madrigals, their dual use was recognized, for on the title-page he describes them as ' apt for the viols and voices '. Later madrigalists followed his example, and Byrd's 1611 set has ' fit for Voyces or Viols ' appended to its title. The same thing had happened in Italy, and Orlando di Lassus used to write at the head of his madrigals ' Buone da cantare e suonare '. It is a short step to go on and write pure string music in which the instruments begin to assert a style of their own. By 1611 Byrd had already taken that step, for in this same volume he includes a fine fantasia in six parts for strings (Gramophone record H.M.V. E293) which had been composed at an earlier date along with numerous *In Nomines*[1] and other fantasias in three, four, five, six, seven, and eight parts.

Instrumental music for the keyboard instruments, virginals, harpsichord and organ, following a somewhat similar course of development had reached about the same stage of growth and emancipation. By the time that Byrd began to write, the use of the virginals was widespread, stimulated no doubt by the example of the Royal performers. It is usually supposed that this little domestic instrument, the true ancestor of the cottage piano, obtained its name from the fact that it was a fashionable accomplishment among young ladies of the time to perform upon it, or them, as contemporary usage preferred to style the instrument. Like scissors the virginals are a single instrument with a grammatical plural number, and are often referred to as a ' paire of virgynalles '. Their use however was not restricted to virgins, though men usually preferred the lute, for Henry VIII himself had a partiality both for playing on them and collecting them. There is rather a pretty story told of Queen Elizabeth and her pride in her skill. Curious

[1] Burney defines an *In Nomine* thus : This was an ancient chant to that part of the Mass beginning *Benedictus qui venit in nomine Domini,* upon which the English masters of the sixteenth century had great delight in exercising their science and ingenuity.

about the personality of Mary Queen of Scots, she asked Melville the Scottish Ambassador a number of very personal questions and invited comparison between herself and her rival. Among them she inquired whether Mary played well. Melville replied : ' Reasonably for a Queen.' The matter could not be left at that. After dinner on the same day Elizabeth contrived to be overheard by Melville playing the virginals. Being caught in the act she affected to be annoyed and ' came forward seeming to strike him with her hand alleging that she used not to play before men, but when she was solitary to shun melancholy.' However, she must needs ask whether she or Mary was the better player, and the courteous but reluctant Melville ' in this was obliged to give her praise '.

There is a virginal that belonged to Queen Elizabeth in the Victoria and Albert Museum. It is a little instrument only 8½ inches in height and 1 foot 11 inches in depth. It has however a length of 5 ft. 5 inches and a range of four octaves. As will be seen from the illustration, it has no stand of its own like the large wing-shaped harpsichords of later times, but was meant to be portable and could be placed on an ordinary table. The principle of the instrument is the plucked string (unlike the piano in which the string is hit with a hammer) and it is derived from the psaltery and the organ. The keyboard was invented for the organ even in antiquity, while the psaltery makes use of the principle of stretching

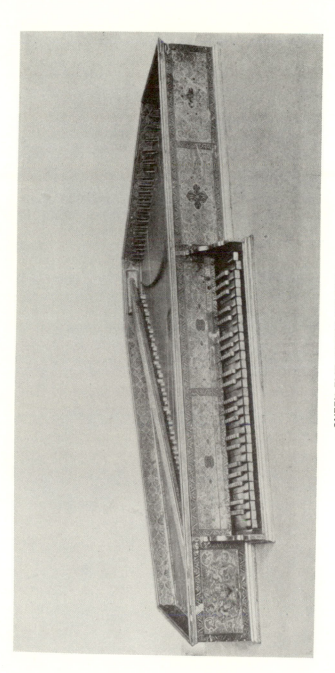

QUEEN ELIZABETH'S VIRGINAL

(*Victoria and Albert Museum*)

[*face p. 26*

strings over a resonant soundboard (unlike the lyre). Put the two mechanisms together and you have the instrument which in varying forms was known as the clavicymbal (in French *clavecin,* in Italian *clavicembalo*), the spinet, the harpsichord and the virginals. The essential feature of this type of instrument is the action by which a jack mounted with quill (Latin *spina,* and so *spinette*) rises and plucks the strings, causing them to emit a sound like the single string of a mandoline when plucked once (not twice as the ordinary technique of mandoline playing requires) ; and it must be noted that no difference could be made between loud and soft, since the only effect of making a *sforzando* would be to break the quill (made of a crow's feather). Hence the ornaments, turns, mordents and the like, which are so common a feature of early keyboard music, were devised to give emphasis and call attention to the notes where the rhythm required it, and the trill was used as a substitute for sustained tone.

There is extant a great mass of music for these instruments dating from about 1560, but though they had a vogue in Henry VIII's youth and earlier, there is very little indeed of the music which must have been written for them during the first part of the century. The manuscript called Thomas Mulliner's Book, which is a compilation made by the organist of St. Paul's Cathedral (date uncertain but perhaps c. 1545), consists mostly of transcriptions for the organ of sacred vocal music, and shows instrumental counterpoint parting from vocal counterpoint and making the rudiments of a style of its own. Even earlier and more striking than this is a Hornepype by Hugh Aston, in which use is made of such purely instrumental devices as figures involving wide skips, the sequential repetition of a figure through a very wide extent of keyboard, a tentative spreading of chords, and a free and easy appearance and disappearance of parts such as occurs in writing nowadays for the piano, when ' doublings ' and ' fillings in ' are freely used according to the exigencies of the moment. Hugh Aston was born back in the fifteenth century and he died in 1522. He wrote music for the church, but his chief title to fame is this piece, which has a pastoral character and shows the beginnings of variation form which Byrd was afterwards to exploit. This and its fellow pieces in two MSS. of the period 1550-70 are the earliest specimens of English instrumental music, and on the strength of it he has been called[1] ' the inventor of instrumental composition in Europe ', to the annoyance of historians who are disinclined to bestow such a title on evidence *ex silentio* and who see in it a style too advanced to have been positively the first music ever written for a keyboard. One other name intervenes in the gap between these shadowy figures and the substantial achievements of Byrd and his contemporaries, Bull, Farnaby and

[1] By Forsyth ; Stanford and Forsyth, *History of Music*, p. 167.

Gibbons—Thomas Tallis, whose chief work lay in another field. The *Fitz William Virginal Book*, of which there will be much to say presently, contains two pieces by Tallis; both are called *Felix namque* and both are dry in manner, uninteresting to modern ears, and employing the devices of the old ecclesiastical counterpoint, but varying them with the various ornaments and quick passage work that properly belong to instrumental style. The longer one is very long (it takes eleven minutes to play) and consists of variations on a plain-song; its value to us is historical and scientific, not æsthetic.

If now we turn to the other big item in the royal expenditure—the Chapel Royal, we find a fee of £40 to the Master of the Children, with some extra allowances for ' largess ' and breakfasts for the children, and £365 for the thirty-two gentlemen ' every one of them 7d. ob. a day ', with eight at a lesser fee, bringing the Officers of the Chapel up to forty-one and the total number of persons employed to 114 and the total expenditure to £2,209 os. 5d. ; though as there is no mention of the boys, and they had to be maintained and taught, this does not represent the whole expenditure upon the royal music. There seems to have been some rivalry among the various collegiate establishments which maintained choirs, to obtain the best singers. For Henry VIII scoured the country in search of singing men and boys and sometimes appropriated choristers from

Wolsey's Chapel, which he thought better provided than his own.[1] Burney further records that the methods of the press-gang were employed to recruit the royal choirs, and he quotes a document as early as 1454 which authorizes the impressing of boys of good build and appearance ('membris naturalibus elegantes') into the service of the king, and he suggests that the emphasis on their good appearance is due to the use made of choirboys for dramatic purposes. This conscription of boys continued all through the Tudor period. Before the dissolution of the monasteries the number of choirs requiring singers must have been very considerable, and even after that upheaval the amount of church music composed shows that there was a great and continuous use of music in all the cathedrals and private chapels of the country. Secular music had at this time only begun tentatively to pursue an existence independently of the Church, and it is more than likely that the religious turmoil turned the minds of composers towards a less contentious outlet for their energies. Folk-song of course there has been since music first began, and it was a constant struggle in the Middle Ages to keep the services of the church clear of tunes that had strong unecclesiastical associations. We know too from the history of some of our own English folk-songs that music must have flourished

[1] Quoted by Pollard, *Henry VIII*, who gives as his authority *Letters and Papers*, ii, 410 and 4024.

in Tudor times with as much vigour among the
people as among the governing classes ; the names
of popular tunes such as *Peg-a-Ramsey* and
Greensleeves are mentioned by Shakespeare. But
it was in the church that the development of the
art into the forms in which we know it after the
year 1600 took place, and it is to Church music
that we must go to discover the state of musical
composition in the first half of the sixteenth
century.

Among the gentlemen of the Chapel Royal
mentioned in Edward VI's list is Thos. Birde,
who has been supposed to be the father of William,
and Thomas Tallis who was certainly his artistic
parent. Tallis is one of the few Tudor musicians
whose name is familiar to the non-musical and
hardly musical public. Everybody knows *Glory
to Thee, my God, this night,* and all who have
attended the morning and evening prayer of the
Church of England know well the familiar rise
and fall of the preces and responses with the
austere but moving cadence at the words
' Because there is none other that fighteth for
us, but only Thou O God.' This setting is the
work of Tallis, and it has retained its place in the
Anglican service through the centuries, though
many other composers, including our own Byrd,
also wrote settings. Tallis is not the first
composer to set music to the English words
of the reformed service, neither is he the
only forerunner of Byrd whose work has to be

considered in estimating Byrd's achievement in this field.

Music is much more dependent on social conditions than appears on the surface, and its changing styles reflect the larger movements of human thought, less clearly perhaps, but no less surely, than religion, politics, or literature. Artistic and political events which are ultimately seen to be related, to be products of the same uprush of energy, do not always happen together in time ; sometimes an artistic revival precedes a period of political or social activity, sometimes political changes bring artistic revolutions in their immediate wake. The Russian Revolution, though it has brought important social changes, has not apparently yet produced an intellectual or artistic counterpart ; rather it ought probably to be regarded as the belated product of the same ferment which in the last part of last century gave to the world Russian literature, the music of Borodine, Rimsky-Korsakoff, Moussorgsky, and Rachmaninoff, and that curious mixture of primitive folk-art and aristocratic sophistication— the Russian ballet. A century ago Beethoven brought into music the feeling which in politics became democracy and individualism. Where Haydn had gracefully acquiesced in the reign of authority, Mozart covertly flirted with freedom of thought (especially in *The Magic Flute*), but Beethoven boldly asserted the right of common humanity to all the human emotions. "Countless millions chant one greeting" he set to music in the Choral Symphony, and on the other hand proclaimed in every note he wrote the right to intense personal conviction. His is the music of assertion. If we go back further we find the mere force of political circumstance introducing a French style into English music merely by restoring an exiled Stuart king to his father's empty throne. When we come to the sixteenth century we begin to feel the political and religious consequences of the great intellectual upheaval of the Renaissance. The music of the Tudor period is affected in two ways. The New Learning, which was the spiritual impetus behind the Protestant Reformation, started also a tendency towards secular music here as it did in Italy, and the English Reformation had immediate and direct effect on church music. No historical event has so intimate a connection with the evolution of music as Henry VIII's separation from Rome.

In 1520 Martin Luther hurled his defiance at the Pope from Wittenberg; in 1525 Henry of England for lack of a son and heir had determined to divorce his Queen, Catherine of Aragon. These two events with all that they symbolized and involved led to the substitution of the English Protestant service for the Roman Catholic Mass. The full story of these changes makes painful reading, and the position of the Gentlemen of the Chapel Royal during the chequered years from

33

1535, when the first Anglican Primer was issued,
until 1588, when with the defeat of the Armada
it became plain that England had become permanently Protestant, was one of terrible difficulty.
For unlike the country clergy the Royal Musicians
could not change their faith by halves, and it was
only because all the Tudor monarchs set a high
value on musical skill and did not assign much
political importance to the religious opinions of
mere musicians, that a *modus vivendi* was found
for them. Byrd himself suffered some inconveni-
ence from remaining a firm Catholic, but seems
never to have been in serious danger, although a
Jesuit Father wrote in 1586 ' We met there [the
house of a Mr Bold], Mr Byrd, the most celebrated
musician and organist of the English nation, who
had been formerly in the Queen's Chapel, and
held in the highest estimation ; but for his
religion he sacrificed everything, both his office
and the Court and all those hopes which are
nurtured by such persons as pretend to similar
places in the dwellings of princes, as steps towards
the increasing of their fortunes.' Byrd however
did not lose his office in the Queen's Chapel, for
the cheque book shows that he was continuously
in the royal service from 1569 till his death in
1623. Still there were difficulties enough for
the composers who lived through the stormiest
period of quick changes in the reigns of Edward
VI and Mary.

A composer who embraced the reformed faith

was John Taverner (c. 1495-c. 1550). His name stands at the head of the list of organists on the panel in the organ loft at Christ Church, Oxford, but he did not remain at Cardinal's College, as it was then called, for more than a year or two. Even during his short stay at Oxford (1526-30) he got into trouble for his heretical tendencies. It is recorded[1] that the particular accusation against him was that he hid the books of one Clarke, a member of the college accused of heresy, in the music-school, but like other musicians, who in these disturbed times escaped paying the penalty of their nonconformity because of their usefulness as musicians, he was pardoned by the Cardinal.

In 1530 Wolsey fell from power and was replaced by Thomas Cromwell, who during the next ten years wrested wealth and power and religious authority from the Church and transferred them to the king. Taverner, who gave up music under pressure of religious conviction, became associated with the Lord Chancellor in the suppression of the monasteries and the persecution of Romanists. Ten years, it will be noted, was sufficient to reverse the rôles of orthodox and heretic. He appears as Cromwell's agent at Boston in Lincolnshire, and there is a ghastly passage in one of his letters (dated Sept. 11th, 1538) to Cromwell[2] describing the burning

[1] Foxe, *Acts and Monuments*.
[2] Quoted in the Introduction to *Tudor Church Music*, vol. I.

of a Black Friar and the 'good' effect it had
had in turning men's hearts from 'idolatry.' His
masses and motets must have been composed
before he left Oxford, since he is said to have
repented afterwards of having set 'Popish'
words to music in his unregenerate days.

His music merits some discussion here in that
' he sums up all the qualities of his precursors and
contemporaries, and expresses all their ideals ', to
quote the words of his modern editors. His
Western Wynde Mass shows a number of these
points.

The musical setting of a service for the church
is from the nature of the case a compromise
between two ideals—the liturgical and the
musical.

The function of music is to deepen the effect
of the words of the liturgy, and strictly speaking
the music should be regarded as a means to that
end, but music is restive whenever it cannot be
treated as an end in itself, and musicians are
always at liberty to argue that the glory of God
can be magnified just as much in musical as in
verbal accents. Through the Middle Ages two
criticisms were brought from time to time against
church music : (*a*) it was too elaborate and
instead of enhancing the words obscured them ;
(*b*) tunes of secular origin were treated contra-
puntally and introduced inappropriate associations. These abuses together with the misplaced
contrapuntal ingenuity which accompanied them

36

finally brought matters to a head, and the Council of Trent, which the Church of Rome called together in 1545 in the vain hope of staving off the Reformation by an internal purge, drew up some rigorous regulations to enforce greater simplicity upon composers, in which it laid down the principle of one syllable to a note. This decree was not passed by the Council till some forty years after Taverner wrote his *Western Wynde* mass, but though the elaborate masses seem to have predominated, to judge from a scathing commentary of Erasmus (1526)[1], simpler masses were in use which moved along at a fair pace without, however, having their phrases of melody tied down too rigidly to the syllables of the text. The *Western Wynde* Mass is of this kind, though in appropriate places such as the Sanctus great long phrases are flung off to a single word. Thus the bass part sings two long scale passages that rise from low G to tenor B. Over this bass the popular tune *The Western Wynde* is sung by the soprano.

THE WESTERN WYNDE

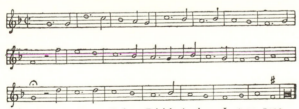

[1] Quoted by Sir Henry Hadow, British Academy Lecture, 1923.

This tune is used thirty-four times, mostly in the soprano part, with different rhythmic arrangements to fit the words of the different sections of the Mass. It has therefore some interest as an early example of a set of variations, more particularly of the musical form known technically as a passacaglia, rather than the air with variations. Byrd uses a similar principle in the motet *Christus Resurgens*[1] (Gradualia I), and in *The Leaves be greene*[2] for strings one and the same tune is continuously present but in different parts. One respect in which Byrd's harmony shows an advance on that of Taverner in this Mass is the *independence* of the parts. In Taverner we find that two parts will often move together at the interval of a third or a sixth. This is a relic of the older system of harmony called faux-bourdon. On the other hand there is plenty of the later contrapuntal device called 'imitation', in which one voice echoes a phrase previously sung by another voice, not necessarily at the same pitch but having the same melodic contour.

Taverner was not the only composer who wrote a Mass round the Western Wynde tune. Indeed, it looks almost as though there was a competition between him and two of his contemporaries similar to the one between Byrd and Ferrabosco, which is described by Thomas Morley, Byrd's pupil, as a 'vertuous contention in love betwixt themselves, made upon the plaine song of

[1] See below, p. 75.　　　　[2] See below, p. 145.

38

Miserere '.[1] At any rate both John Shepherd and Christopher Tye, who were his juniors, wrote Masses based on the same tune, and managed to do it in fewer repetitions of the melody. Both these composers wrote settings of the new English service, which marks the next stage in the English Reformation and a new one in the history of English music.

The musical career of Tye, who adopted the Reformed faith and ultimately took orders (1560), completely covers the transition from the Latin to the English order of service. Fuller writes of him : ' Music, which received a grievous wound in England at the dissolution of abbeys, was much beholding to him for her recovery ; such his excellent skill and piety that he kept it up in credit at court and at all cathedrals during his life.' He seems to have set Latin words long after he had abandoned the Romish faith, but in his work for the English service he adopted a very simple and direct style.[2] Many composers of the period set both languages without having in view their performance in the corresponding ritual. As we shall see, Byrd wrote a vast mass of Latin church music as well as a smaller but still quite considerable amount of music for the English service during the ever-increasing Protestantism of

[1] See below, p. 82.

[2] An Offertory and an Anthem by him are quoted by Wooldridge, Oxford History, Vol. II, pp. 343-349, in which he uses a note against note style such as would allow the words to be clearly intelligible—a point of great concern to the Reformers.

Elizabeth's reign. Tye's claim to remembrance, however, is as one of the first composers of anthems, and as the author of a setting (originally intended not for church use but to be accompanied upon the lute) of the *Actes of the Apostles translated into Englyshe Metre, and dedicated to the kyngs most excellent majestye.* This was the only work he published (1553), and some of the tunes he employed survive in use as psalm tunes. He seems to have been a man of strong personality, with a sharp tongue ; he certainly taught Edward VI and possibly (though there is no evidence for it beyond the fact that Henry VIII thought highly of him) also the Princesses Mary and Elizabeth.

The English language was introduced into the services of the church after the Act of Supremacy of 1534. Ten years later the complete recasting of the liturgy was taken in hand, and Archbishop Cranmer wrote to the king a letter expressing the view that music was admissible for the new rites but that it must be of ' a solemn note ', not florid like the great contrapuntal settings of the Mass, but ' as near as may be for every syllable a note so that it may be sung distinctly and devoutly '. A communion service was substituted for the Mass at Cranmer's suggestion, but it was not till the second year of Edward VI that the *First Book of Common Prayer* appeared, and during the last years of Henry's reign there was some slight persecution of Protestantism, in spite of Cranmer's leanings towards it. Official England was more concerned with the political side of the separation from Rome than with the change of doctrine with which the spreading waves of Lutheranism were beginning to flood the land. But the use of the vernacular in the services, aided as it was by the accessibility of the new English Bible, had taken firm root, and Edward VI's reign saw great activity among the musicians in adapting old plain-song tunes and settings of the Mass and motets into the English form of service and anthems. In 1550 John Merbecke published his *The Booke of Common Prayer Noted*, in which Matins, Evensong, and the Communion and Burial services are set to adaptations of plain-song melodies. He had narrowly escaped being burned at the stake for heresy in 1540, when, as we have seen, there was an attempt to prevent reforming zeal from going beyond its political boundaries into the realm of religion. He was, however, reprieved, possibly because he was a musician, and he retained the organistship of St George's, Windsor, even during the Roman persecution, which seems to have left him unscathed. Perhaps he had learned discretion and like most other organists found that it was possible to carry out his musical duties without doing violence to his private religious beliefs.

The second Prayer Book of Edward VI was first issued in 1552, and it was adopted in 1559 after Elizabeth's accession. Provision was made also for the singing of hymns and anthems provided that they were always such that their words were readily intelligible. In 1560 John Day issued a collection of settings for the re-established Anglican services, including the Communion service. Anthems were made out of Latin motets refitted with English words, and new motets were composed to words from the Bible. The old form of service did not disappear altogether from private chapels of Catholic nobles like Byrd's patron, the Earl of Worcester. But as time went on Protestantism became firmly established, owing partly to the dying out of the old priesthood, partly to the Puritan tendencies which began to arise and to attract the allegiance of the sturdy middle classes, and partly to the odium which the religious persecution on the continent brought on Catholicism. By 1579 the Queen was in a strong enough position to enforce the Act of Uniformity, and we hear of prosecutions for ' recusancy ' and non-attendance at church. The resentment roused by the Armada still further stiffened the feeling against Rome and all its ways. Yet Byrd at any rate continued to write Latin Church music, including three Masses and a vast quantity of motets, and to publish it in the even more Protestant reign of James.

In tracing the musical effects of the English Reformation it has so happened that we have seen how composers who turned Protestant fared. The Protestantism of Taverner caused him to give up music and it is possible that Tye followed the

42

same course, though there is a composition of his
—a Latin one too—dated 1568. Marbecke
continued both his musical and his theological
activities. But many remained Catholics all
their lives—Shepherd (c. 1511-1562), Mundy
(c. 1515-1591), Byrd himself, and his immediate
predecessor, Thomas Tallis, whose work forms the
chief foundations on which Byrd built.

At the dissolution of the greater monasteries in
1540 Tallis was organist of Waltham Abbey. He
was paid 20 shillings for wages and 20 shillings
as a gratuity, and soon joined the Chapel Royal,
which appointment he held through all the
religious changes of the time until his death in
1585. Beside the Preces and Responses, his
services in the Dorian Mode and the Litany were
composed for use in the liturgy of Edward VI's
second Prayer Book. A few years later five
anthems of his were included in the collection of
John Day, and nine metrical tunes were written
for Archbishop Parker's *Psalter* in 1567. His
work for the English ritual is plain (as it was bound
to be to meet ecclesiastical requirements) to the
point of severity, and in the beautiful little anthem,
O Lord, give Thy Holy Spirit, there is an austerity
even greater than one finds in Byrd, who is notable
for the same quality. When he set Latin words,
however, he allowed himself greater freedom, and
in a famous motet indulged in an orgy of contrapuntal ingenuity. ' The most curious and extraordinary of all his labours ', says Burney, ' was

his *Song of Forty Parts*, which is still subsisting,
This wonderful effort of harmonical abilities is
not divided into choirs of four parts . . .
but consists of eight trebles placed under each
other ; eight mezzi-soprani or mean parts ;
eight counter-tenors ; eight tenors ; and eight
basses ; with one line allotted to the organ. All
these several parts, as may be imagined, are not in
simple counterpoint, or filled up in mere harmony,
without meaning or design, but have each a share
in the short subjects of fugue and imitation,
which are introduced upon any change of words.
. . . Thus all the forty real[1] parts are severally
introduced in the course of 39 bars, when the
whole vocal phalynx is employed at once during
six bars more. . . . And thus this stupendous
though perhaps Gothic, specimen of human labour
and intellect, is carried on in alternate flight,
pursuit, attack and choral union to the end ;
when the *Polyphonic Phenomenon* is terminated
by twelve bars of universal chorus, in quad-
ragintesimal harmony.'

For the sake of Burney's piquant commentary
the attention which might with greater propriety
be given to the Latin Church music has been
spent on this musical tour de force.[2] Many of

---

[1] Dr. Walker says : ' I can recollect no other instance of music (worthy
the name) in even half this number of real parts, sixteen is the practical
limit.' Dr. Walker is also emphatic in regarding it as a work of art and not
as a mere puzzle.

[2] This work has been performed recently in King's College Chapel,
Cambridge, under Dr. A. H. Mann.

his Latin motets were adapted for use as English anthems, but sixteen of the most important of them were published in the volume of *Cantiones quae ab argumento Sacrae vocantur, quinque et sex partium*,[1] which he issued jointly with Byrd in 1575. He wrote also settings of the *Lamentations* in which there is a dignity and resignation which have suggested to some that there is personal feeling behind the sorrows of the music in which the composer regrets the pass to which the music of the church had come. If the work was composed in 1580, he might well feel uneasy at the onslaughts of the Puritans, who complained that the service ' of God is grievously abused by piping with organs, singing, ringing and trowling of Psalms from one side of the choir to another, with the squealing of chanting choristers.'[2] What is even more significant of his own feeling is that after his early essays he seems to have abandoned composition for the English liturgy altogether.

One more branch of music demands a glance before this long chapter can be closed. The first set of English madrigals to be published was the *Psalms Sonnets and Songs* of Byrd in 1588. But they did not fall out of a clear sky. *Ex nihilo nihil fit* is, if possible, more rigorously true of music than of anything else, and that in spite of

---

[1] Songs called Sacred from the nature of their subject, in five and six parts.

[2] This citation (quoted from Burney) is from a pamphlet of rather later date, but the Puritan agitation had begun ten years or more before this.

music being called with sober truth a creative art. Every composer has a forerunner and every important innovation has been tried before—or something like it. Madrigal singing came from Italy, and we have no need to grope for its origins among our own secular song-making. Italy was the cultural centre of the world at this time, and in Italy the composers, who derive from the great Flemish school and through them ultimately from John Dunstable (the Englishman who won more fame and influence abroad than in England), had been writing madrigals for half a century before English composers seriously began to think of secular music for amateurs beside the ecclesiastical music for the professional choirs which they directed. Until this happened the amateurs imported their madrigals from Italy and sang the Italian words. Dr. Fellowes describes a set of part-books in the library of Winchester College which date from 1564 and contain nearly a hundred French and Italian songs in four parts. The dedication of *Musica Transalpina*, a collection of Italian madrigals published in 1588, throws an interesting side-light upon the practice of madrigal singing by amateurs and shows what a vogue this delightful pastime had already obtained. Nicholas Yonge, the editor of this work, which was provided with a literal translation set alongside of the Italian words, tells how he was wont to gather together at his house in St. Michael's Cornhill (still a place where musicans of the City foregather) ' a great number of Gentlemen and Merchants of good accompt (as well of this realme as of forreine nations) ' for the ' exercise of Musicke daily '. He used to obtain for them the latest publications from Italy, a fact which has led Burney to call him an Italian merchant who from the nature of his business had special facilities for obtaining the best continental productions. Dr. Fellowes, however, identifies him with a lay-clerk of St Paul's. In this collection he included two madrigals by Byrd which are settings of two stanzas of Ariosto's *La Virginella*, thus setting an English composer on an equality with the Italian masters.

Though Italian music undoubtedly predominated at these music parties there are a few madrigals of English origin prior to the year 1588. Of these the best known is *In going to my naked bed*, of which the words are certainly by Richard Edwards and the music ascribed with probability to him.[1] This work is found in the Mulliner MS, while the words come from the *Paradyse of Dainty Devises*, where other verses beside the one usually sung are written round the theme ' The falling out of faithful friends renewing is of love '. This madrigal is of the most exquisite charm, very smooth in character, with harmonies somewhat less astringent than is characteristic of Byrd.

---

[1] Edwardes was a musician with other contributions to his credit ; the only authority which seriously questions his authorship of this madrigal is *The Oxford History*, which attributes it to Tye.

Though it contains points of imitation, it is less contrapuntal and more homophonic than the later madrigals. Edwards was a court poet as well as musician and wrote for Elizabeth plays to be performed by the children of the Chapel Royal as well as Latin motets for Queen Mary. His song *When griping grief* is quoted by Shakespeare in *Romeo and Juliet*, and a song for two trebles, alto and tenor called *By painted wordes* is sometimes heard. There is a blitheness, a delicacy and a vigour about his work both as poet and musician, very characterisic of his age, which earned for him the posthumous eulogy, 'the flower of all our realm and Phœnix of our age'.

The earliest known set of part-books was published by Wynkyn de Worde in 1530, which contained twenty madrigals. But instances of secular songs of an earlier date are to be found in MSS, usually with a simple harmonic accompaniment for other voices, composed by Robert Fayrfax and William Cornysh (both of whom accompanied Henry VIII to the Field of the Cloth of Gold) and other less notable men. The dramatic entertainments for which the Chapel Royal was responsible were productive of a certain amount of song writing, and even composers of so severe an outlook as Tye and Tallis have left examples of secular polyphony. Robert Fayrfax left a book (believed to be in his own hand) of secular music containing sixty-three vocal and forty-nine instrumental pieces. We have therefore the *Fayrfax MS* from the early part of the

48

century; we have also the compositions of King Henry VIII himself, and we have the printed collection of madrigals of Wynkyn de Worde; then there is a gap, at the end of which the Mulliner MS reveals traces of the secular music of a date between the end of Henry VIII's reign and the accession of Elizabeth; and finally we come to Thomas Whythorne, who published a set of part books entitled *Songes of three fouer and five voyces* in 1571, which contained no less than seventy-six madrigals. This seems to be the tale of eighty years work by British composers in the field of secular music. The next forty-five years was to see pouring from the press a continuous stream of vocal music of the very highest quality, which ended almost as suddenly as it began. Byrd's *Psalms Sonnets and Songs* marks the beginning of the Golden Age of English music.

CHAPTER III

BYRD was born in 1543. At the age of twenty
he was appointed organist at Lincoln cathedral,
where he remained some half a dozen years. He
was therefore too young at the time of the
religious upheavals of the middle of the century
to be involved personally in them, and when he
took up his appointment at Lincoln the English
liturgy was established but was desperately poor
in music for the canticles. Authority had not
precluded music in the reformed service and
Puritan zeal had not yet risen up to eject it, so
that there was scope for a young composer to
provide services, anthems, and settings of the
Preces and Responses—here was pioneer work
crying out to be done. Byrd set to and did it,
for there can be little doubt that he had written
important work for the English church before he
was appointed to the Chapel Royal at the age of
twenty-six. And not only English service music
but Latin as well. For six years later, soon after
he went to London, he published in association
with Tallis a volume of *Cantiones quae ab argumento sacræ vocantur* which contained sixteen
motets of Tallis and eighteen of Byrd. Tallis
was some thirty years older than Byrd, so that
the mere fact of their association marks Byrd out

as a man of uncommon ability and classes him with Tallis as a 'parent of English Music'. The disciple thus imitated the master in the practice of writing both Latin and English church music side by side, a practice he maintained throughout his life. Although the opportunities for the use of Latin music were limited—some of it was doubtless sung domestically like the madrigals— Byrd's writings in this field far outnumber his English church compositions. It is just worth noting that in this early publication there is an example of a musical puzzle such as all the great masters of the technique of composition following Tallis, have delighted to set themselves to solve. The motet *Diliges Dominum* is a canon in which one choir of four voices sings the same music as a second choir but backwards. The words are printed underneath the music in the ordinary way and also upside-down above the staff; over each part is written: *Duae partes in una recte & retro* (two parts in one straight forward and backwards). This kind of simultaneous equation requires some little ingenuity.

The word 'motet' has already been used repeatedly; it is time to define it. Unfortunately it is one of those terms which refuse to behave strictly, and at different periods it encroaches on its neighbours' territory. Originally it was the music sung at High Mass while the priest was preparing the bread and wine and consecrating them at the altar. It was thus a piece of

unaccompanied choral music of moderate length
set to Latin words taken from the Bible or the
Office books of the church. The anthem of the
reformed service was a rough equivalent to it, and
later it came to be applied to any piece of choral
music which was (*a*) set to serious words in any
language and (*b*) was unaccompanied. Finally
the term was loosely applied to accompanied vocal
works of a serious character. In Elizabethan
times it meant any piece of music which was
suitable for performance at the Mass or at the
festivals of the church ; and though many of
Byrd's motets must have been sung as madrigals
since there were no public celebrations of the
Roman service, the term is reserved not merely
for compositions in a certain style (its present
rather indefinite meaning) but for settings of
Latin words.

After this early volume of *Cantiones Sacræ*,
Byrd's next publication was his first volume of
madrigals in 1588, followed by *Songs of Sundrie
Natures* in 1589. In the same year he published
a further volume of *Cantiones Sacræ*, this time
consisting entirely of his own work, and followed
it in 1591 with a second book. Then comes a
rather mysterious break in his musical activity, and
nothing more of his appears until 1605, when he
published another collection of music with Latin
words. This is the first book of the *Gradualia*,
followed two years later by a second book. In the
second edition of this second book of *Gradualia*

published in 1610 Byrd's three Masses appear to have been surreptitiously circulated, as in the few surviving copies they are found interleaved between the motets and have no date or title page of their own. The date of their composition, as indeed of most of Byrd's church music, is unknown.[1] In 1611 *Parthenia* appeared, a collection of pieces for the virginals by Byrd, Bull, and Gibbons, and the same year saw the publication of his last set of madrigals. This is the sum total of his published work. His output of Latin ecclesiastical music amounts to three Masses and about 230 motets and kindred choral works. In mere bulk it demands first consideration as the largest category and in quality it is usually regarded as his supreme achievement.

The listener whose only experience of contrapuntal music is the massive works of Handel or Bach with their orchestral accompaniment, approaching Elizabethan music for the first time, would do well to begin (especially if he is approaching it at one remove from reality through a gramophone) not with the brilliant compositions in five, six, or eight parts, but with such a work as the three-part Mass of Byrd. If he listens with his ears focussed to the range required for Bach and Handel Elizabethan music in a large number of parts will sound like a confused babel without the grandeur of the more solid music, and it will take him a little time to

[1] For such evidence as there is see Dr. Fellowes's *William Byrd*, p. 32.

make the adjustment necessary to perceive the order and symmetry in this kaleidoscope of tunes as they dissolve from one voice to another. It will not take him long however to stop down his ears until he gets three lines of sinuous melody focussed sharply. As in an etching where economy of line yields a maximum of meaning, he will perceive the three parts mingling without losing the identity and individual significance of each. And if he is curious about the way things work, after finding its beauty, he can see for himself the manner and method of contrapuntal composition, though the mysteries of its technique, with its curious prohibitions and to our ears even more curious licences, he may well leave to a curiosity hardier than his own. Two movements of the Three-part Mass, the *Kyrie* and the *Sanctus*, are recorded for the gramophone (H.M.V. E290) by the English Singers, and the complete Mass is published with a condensed pianoforte score (by Stainer and Bell, price 1s. 6d.). The *Kyrie* is a very beautiful little movement with the main interest in the top part (the alto—the other two being a tenor and a bass). There is no repetition of the words and there is no great elaboration of separate syllables until the final *e-lei-son*. *Kyrie eleison*[1] the voices sing quietly together in homophonic[2] style. *Christe eleison* they sing a little

[1] Greek for ' Lord have mercy '—a curious Greek survival in a Latin text.
[2] Homophonic, from Greek ὁμός = common or joint, and φωνή = voice, means harmonic as opposed to contrapuntal in style ; the voices strike their notes together.

louder to the same fragment of tune though the lower parts have changed ; and then more quietly than ever they sing the third short phrase with its little melismatic[1] passage to signify a gentle insistence. That is all, and there is nothing to strike the unaccustomed ear as extraordinary except that in the simplicity of the harmony there is a peculiar beauty. It is, however, unusual to find a three-fold *Kyrie* ; at this time a nine-fold *Kyrie* was customary. The *Gloria* begins with the same phrase as the *Kyrie*, altered only so far as to carry the new words. The same device is employed at the beginnings of the *Benedictus* and the *Agnus Dei*. This is not quite the same principle as either recapitulation or leit-motif used by later composers to give unity to a composition. But it has a unifying effect while allowing new material to grow out of a common root. In this movement melismatic phrases are used for the words *cælestis* (heavenly) and *Christe*. At the words *miserere nobis* (have mercy upon us) all the voices cease together and there is a silence. The words which follow are *Quoniam tu solus sanctus* (Since thou alone art holy) and to give an emphatic certitude to the assertion the voices resume unanimously in block harmony. There is a very lovely *Amen* in thirds given first to the lower two voices and then to the upper two, while the third voice in each case sings a

---

[1] Melismatic, from Greek μέλος = melody, means a little flourish of florid melody.

sustained phrase. A similar effect is employed at the end of the *Sanctus*. In the *Credo* there is a homophonic passage for the words *Et in unum Dominum* (And in one Lord) while the words singled out for melodic emphasis are *Jesu*, and *vero* (true, or in the customary phrase 'very God of very God'), and again *coelis* (the heavens). There is a beautiful harmonic touch to signify the mystery of the incarnation at the word incar*n*atus, when on the italicized syllable a D flat is sounded for the first time in the whole Mass, which is almost continuously in the key of E flat[1] with its closely related neighbours on the sharp side of the key. This descent on to the flat side of the key which is technically called a modulation to the subdominant, gives the impression of being suddenly cast into deeper waters. The previous phrase ended on the tonic chord of the predominant key in its strongest, i.e., its root, position. *Et incarnatus* begins on the chord of A flat, which is of course a chord in the key of E flat viz. the diatonic chord on the fourth degree, but with the introduction of the crucial note, D flat, the modulation is made and is continued into the relative minor key, F minor, in which the music remains until the words *homo factus est* (and was made man), where the return to normal non-mysterious things is marked by a return to the normal E flat major. The resurrection and ascension are naturally portrayed in

[1] The original pitch was a tone higher.

ascending passages, the one in a crisp theme of five notes, the other in a long ascending scale, which are not the pictorial crudities one might think but do very suggestively convey the effects of soaring and renewed vitality. The *Amen* of this section very ingeniously recalls these phrases without imitating them and furthermore fore-shadows the *Sanctus*. Even at the risk of carrying technical analysis too far, the *Sanctus* must be studied in closer detail, since it can be obtained for reproduction on the gramophone where it can be heard over and over again and examined closely. It is one long crescendo both of feeling and of tone leading up to triumphant cries of *Osanna in excelsis*. It begins quietly and in order that the beginning shall be as little exciting as possible all three voices enter close on one another's heels on the same note, E flat. The actual shape of the phrases to which the word 'sanctus' (holy) is set is like a fine springing arch, in whose upward thrust there is a latent exaltation. Two voices use these phrases against the sustaining long notes of the third voice. Each voice repeats the word 'sanctus' three times, and they come to a close together. These frequent full closes ('cadences' as they are called) are a characteristic of the music of the period during which the principles of musical structure were only beginning to emerge; as in the madrigals the shape and size of the musical phrase is determined entirely by the verbal phrases. *Dominus Deus Sabaoth*

(Lord God of Sabaoth) is the next short phrase ; it is given out more loudly, the voices following each other in with the effect of increased urgency which is made by the use of the contrapuntal device called the *stretto* (a word meaning ' contracted ' and applied to passages in which the voices anticipate their proper entries and come in tumbling over one another). *Pleni sunt cœli* (The heavens are full) has a phrase which the alto sings first and which is then imitated by the bass, the tenor in the meanwhile singing the same phrase but with its rhythm so distorted as to make it sound like a counter-subject.[1] The alto and bass sing *gloria tua* (of Thy Glory) together in tenths while the tenor answers it antiphonally. With *Osanna in excelsis* (Hosanna in the heights) Byrd returns to an idea somewhat similar to his opening phrase (sanctus) and works it up to a tremendous climax by making all the voices climb into their high registers and then gradually descend in a beautiful curve into the middle where their tone is strongest, the voices being used in pairs again here. The *Benedictus* and the *Agnus Dei* are quiet movements which start from the same opening phrase, and the Mass ends, as is appropriate to the words *dona nobis pacem* (give us peace), on a note of severity but great simplicity.

---

[1] The main tunes of a contrapuntal composition are technically called subjects—the counter-subject is the theme sung *against* the first tune, which it sets off by contrast.

I have gone into this Mass at some length for the sake of any reader energetic enough to procure a score and to look into it at the piano or in the jaws of his gramophone, because an understanding of the way this Elizabethan music is built is a help to the appreciation of its restrained and subtle beauties. The other Masses must be passed over more briefly. One number of the four-part Mass—the *Agnus Dei*—is sung fairly frequently by parties of madrigal singers and has been recorded for gramophone (H.M.V. E290—the other side of the three-part Mass record). Taken as a whole this Mass is more elaborate than the three-part Mass, and takes slightly longer in performance. Even before the edict of the Council of Trent (1563), which sought to simplify the liturgy and clear it of some of the far-fetched contrapuntal ingenuities which quite buried the words and the sense which they sought to convey, it seems to have been the practice of composers to provide two kinds of settings of the Mass, the one more or less direct and without undue repetition of the words, the other, reserved probably for high festivals, set out upon an altogether bigger scale in which the composer's imagination had free play and made the words subordinate to their musical intentions. The three-part Mass belongs definitely to the first kind, and though the four-part Mass is not unduly elaborate, the words are freely repeated in order to fill out the musical design. The *Kyrie* for example, consists of three sections each with a close of its own, not three phrases, and the soprano sings the words 'kyrie eleison' when they come the second time six times over. The *Agnus Dei* begins with a duet for the two upper voices, which colours the words with tender feeling. It is not till the eighth measure that the two lower parts enter, and it is noteworthy how the chord of A flat is gradually built up by the overlapping of the parts. On the word 'nobis' (*miserere nobis* have mercy upon us) Byrd employs again the method already noticed of using the voices in pairs in parallel tenths which gives to the passage a kind of personal appeal, and if one compares the general feeling of this movement with Handel's setting of the same words (only in English) one cannot but be struck by the greater intimacy of the Catholic composer as compared with the wider social prayer of the Protestant. The traditional rôles of these great churches are reversed : the Roman prays that the Lamb of God may have mercy on his own sins, the plural 'us' being used because many are taking part at the same time in the same intercession, while the whole feeling of Handel's music, based as it is on a slightly different version of the same words ('*Behold* the lamb of God which taketh away the sins of the world' without the further phrase 'Have mercy upon us') is of a corporate salvation revealed majestically to the whole world. It is one of the secrets of the age-old words of the Mass that differences of

60

aspect of this kind reveal themselves to different composers in different ages, and make it possible for new inspiration to clothe itself in new forms in the minds of men like Bach and Vaughan Williams, who are not Roman Catholics at all. As the movement proceeds there is an increase of intensity, obtained not by any crescendo but by a closer weaving of the parts. The same feeling of tenderness and quietness with which the two voices began prevails to the end, and indeed *dona nobis pacem* is sung over and over again each time more quietly than the last, yet seeming to become more and more charged with feeling. The whole movement grows on one with repeated hearings; it is both ethereal and strong—qualities which maybe it gets from the exceptional combination of firmness with mobility in the bass part.

It is a characteristic of this kind of music that ' points ' do not stick out of it, and commentary on isolated details (when they can be isolated) may induce a wrong frame of mind in the listener, and restrain him from yielding himself to the flow of the music in the hope of catching some special feature. But though there are plenty of differences of mood in Byrd's writings, it is chiefly by points of detail that these works which are so alike in style can be differentiated. In this Mass one may call attention to the melisma on the word ' cœlis ' again and to the complicated interlacing of phrases of ' cujus regni non erit finis' (p. 22, whose kingdom knows no end). The *Osanna* of the *Benedictus* too is a remarkable piece of counterpoint, which grows more florid as it increases in loudness and comes finally to a curious cadence which gives the impression of the whole thing dissolving into clouds of glory.

The five-part Mass is more elaborate, though Byrd never goes far from the principle of a syllable to a note except in the case of the special words which he selects here as in the other Masses for melismatic treatment. But from the nature of the case a greater splendour of effect is possible. The voices are used sparingly and sing all together only at climaxes or special important words like 'Quoniam tu solus' or 'et unam sanctam catholicam et apostolicam ecclesiam', but antiphonal use of groups of voices adds greatly to the resources of expression. The *Sanctus* is a fine number made up of short vigorous phrases, and other points worth noting are a bright modulation to the dominant at 'lumen de lumine' (light of light) and the curious sense of lightness at the words 'tollis peccata mundi' by the modulation up one degree to the supertonic—the removal of the sins has as it were made the music more buoyant. Byrd has given a more unescapable feeling of unity to this Mass than to the others by the insistent use of the same opening phrase and by a partiality for a plagal form of cadence, highly ornamented but even in its ornamentation keeping

as a constant figure the little formula called
'changing notes'.

Most of the other Latin Church music is
contained in the five collections which Byrd
published during his own life. There are however, some fifty motets still in manuscript, and a
few canons including the famous *Non nobis Domine*,
which is ascribed to him without much evidence.
This little work consists of only twenty-two bars ;
the second voice enters a fourth below in the
second bar, the third at the fourth bar an octave
below. There is a story that there is a copy of it
engraved in gold in the Vatican, to which an
allusion is made in a complimentary poem to
Dr Blow of the late seventeenth century. Dr
Pepusch, of *Beggar's Opera* fame, in a treatise on
harmony of the year 1730, unhesitatingly calls it
' the famous canon by William Byrd'. And
Boyce in the Introduction to his *Cathedral Music*
says ' His canon of *Non nobis Domine* will in
particular remain a perpetual monument to his
memory.' As there are no other serious claimants
the ascription must go by default to Byrd.[1] The
first collection of motets which Byrd published in
collaboration with Tallis in 1575 has already been
mentioned. The full title was *Cantiones Quæ*

[1] Other evidence, not conclusive, but pointing to Byrd's authorship, is
the inclusion of the canon under Byrd's name in Playford's *Musical Banquet*
of 1651, its ascription to him by Mattheson (1739), and its occurrence on the
title page of a MS. copy of *Gradualia* in the Ewing Library, Glasgow (1774).
See a letter from Dr. Grattan Flood in *The Times Literary Supplement*,
Sept. 6, 1923.

Ab | *Argumento Sacrae Vocantur, Quinque et Sex Partium, Autoribus* | *Thoma Tallisio* & *Guilielmo Birdo Anglis, Serenis* | *simæ Regineæ Maiestati a privato Sacello ge* | *nerosis et Organistis* (Cum privilegio) Excudebat Thomas Vautrollerius typographus Londiniensis in claustro vulgo Blackfriers commorans 1575 (Songs which from the nature of their subject-matter are called sacred, of five and six parts, by Thomas Tallis and William Byrd, Englishmen, gentlemen and organists to the Queen's most Serene Majesty in her private Chapel.) As Byrd entitled his next two publications of Latin music *Cantiones Sacræ*, the elaborate phrase 'quae ab argumento vocantur' is a useful distinguishing mark. Two other small points emerge from this title. Byrd was joint organist with Tallis. Burney says that boy-organists were not appointed before the reign of Elizabeth and that Tye and Blithman, Tallis, and Byrd are the earliest laymen recorded in the post. 'Cum privilegio' refers to the monopoly in music printing which the composers enjoyed, to which further reference is made below (pp. 210 seq.). In 1588 and 1589 Byrd published two volumes of madrigals ; the two books of *Cantiones Sacræ* came out in 1589 and 1591. The title of the 1589 collection is : *Liber Primus* | *Sacrarum Cantio* | *num Quinque vocum.* | Autore | Guilielmo Byrd Organista | Regio, Anglo | Excudebat Thomas Est ex assigna | tione Guilielmi Byrd. | Cum privilegio. | Londini. 25. Octob. 1589 (The first book of Sacred Songs of five voices by William Byrd the Royal Organist, Englishman. Printed by Thomas East at the assignation of William Byrd, etc.). Again the printer's name is of some interest, and this assignation will be discussed in its proper place (p. 212). Since the time of publication was late autumn we may perhaps assume that Byrd brought out his first volume of English music, the 1588 set of madrigals, before issuing what is after all his second publication of Latin music. In this collection we may select for comment four numbers. These motets are often in two or more parts, which makes for confusion in naming and numbering them. Thus *Ne irascaris* (Be not wroth) and *Civitas sancti tui* (the city of Thy Holy place) are really two parts of a single motet, but they are known as two separate English anthems, being among the works adapted during Byrd's own lifetime for the new liturgy. *Lord in thy wrath* and *Bow Thine Ear* were printed by Barnard in 1641 in his collection, and along with *Sing joyfully unto God* were printed in the more famous eighteenth-century collection of Boyce. *Bow Thine Ear* is one of the few works of Byrd which has been continuously in the cathedral repertory from Byrd's own day till ours. Being well known in this form it may more conveniently be discussed among the English Church music.[1] Its mournful character, however, represents the general tone of this collection, and is

[1] See below, p. 101.

5

so marked as to suggest[1] that these motets express, more specifically than is usual in a composer's works, his personal feelings about the state into which his well-loved religion had fallen by this time. For Protestantism, with Puritanism hard on its heels, increased in strength steadily through Elizabeth's reign, and with the defeat of the Armada (1588) and the hardening of opinion against the Roman religion which it brought about, faithful Catholics like Byrd may well have despaired of the revival of the faith to which in the strength of their devotion they had pinned their hopes. *In resurrexione*, however, is naturally in a joyous mood, and so is *O quam gloriosum*,† which shows in its two parts the long sweeping phrases characteristic of Byrd. The harmonies hover within a rather narrow range, but the florid forward movement and the swaying of the parts produce an exhilaration almost like that of change-ringing of bells which the composer frequently uses for the expression of joy and exaltation. Indeed it is even more marked in *Lætentur Cæli*† (Let the heavens be glad), another motet in the same volume. A more striking motet is *Vigilate nescitis enim*† (Be watchful for ye know not), which is built of terse, vigorous phrases and is full of descriptive word painting, which does not

---

[1] Mr. H. B. Collins ventures this opinion and discusses Byrd's Latin Church music in a paper read to the Musical Association. See Mus. Assoc. Proceedings, 39th session.

† Published in a cheap edition by the Oxford University Press.

however hold up the march of the music or in the slightest degree impair the unity of the whole. The words are : ' Be ye watchful, for ye know not when the Lord shall come to his house, whether late or in the middle of the night or at cock-crow, or in the morning ; be watchful therefore lest when he suddenly cometh, he findeth you sleeping. And what I say to you I say to all men, be watchful'. To the word 'sero' (late) is assigned a little drooping phrase, which is imitated in all five parts suggesting the closing in of night ; cockcrow (an galli cantu) is painted in a strong uprising phrase 3¾ bars in length in its full form :

This is not realism—it is not nearly so close to the bird's cry as the little figures in Bach's *Passions*—

yet it has an assertive triumphant ring that is extraordinarily suggestive of the natural phenomenon. The same phrase reshaped (quite in the manner of a Wagnerian motif) to a broader, less exciting mould serves to carry on the idea of the plain daylight of morning. At the word 'repente' (suddenly) there is an alarming rush of semi-quavers grouped in a scale passage followed by insistent knocking :

over and over again. The drowsiness of the sleeper appears thus :

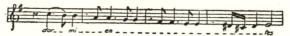

The work ends with emphatic reiterations of 'vigilate.'

The second book of *Cantiones Sacrae* is entitled : *Liber Secundus | Sacrarum Cantionum | Quarum aliae ad Quinque, aliae veroad | Sex voces aeditae sunt.* | (The second book of sacred songs, of which some are arranged for five and others for six voices.) The remainder of the title page reads as for the first volume, except that the date is " quarto Novemb. 1591." This volume contains *Exsurge Domine*[1] (Arise, O Lord, why sleepest thou), not perhaps one of the most attractive of Byrd's motets, but showing the peculiar nobility of style characteristic of the composer, which grows on one. The texture is a good deal tighter than Byrd usually employs with five voices, which in this case sing all together for most of the time. The result is a certain massiveness to which a touch of grace is added

[1] Gramophone, H.M.V. D710.

by two lovely little points, both in the soprano part : (1) the little ornament on the word ' nostræ ' before the return of ' exsurge ' and (2) the unexpected rise to the last note of all, which, besides making a musical climax, has the poetical significance that the Lord has risen at last in answer to the prayer. Other motets in the 1591 set which are accessible in a cheap edition are *Miserere mei*, an example of Byrd's mastery in handling a sober and subdued style, and *Cantate Domino*, a big six-part work, very complicated rhythmically, which builds up to a tremendous climax of exultation.[1] *Hæc Dies* (This is the day which the Lord hath made) for six voices must be distinguished from the less striking setting for five voices in the second book of *Gradualia*. It is full of Easter joy, contains a beautiful change of rhythm to suggest dancing at the word *lætemur* (let us be glad), and builds up a climax by a five-fold rising sequence.

Between the last book of the *Cantiones* in 1591 and the first of the *Gradualia* in 1605 Byrd published nothing, but as before followed up one book by the speedy publication of a second of the same kind of work, the second book of *Gradualia* in 1607. *Gradualia* means settings of the movable (i.e. proper to the day) parts of the Mass, viz. the Introit, Gradual, Offertory and Communion (Gradual in this more limited sense means the

---

[1] Both edited by Miss Townsend Warner for the *Tudor Church Music Series* (Oxford University Press, price 4d. each).

Respond between the Epistle and the Gospel), as opposed to the fixed parts of the Mass, the *Kyrie*, the *Gloria in Excelsis*, the *Credo*, the *Sanctus* and the *Agnus Dei*. Byrd's first book of *Gradualia* contains provision for the festivals of the Blessed Virgin, All Saints, and Corpus Christi, besides a few miscellaneous pieces of which the words come from the Breviary; the second book covers Christmas, Epiphany, Easter, Ascension, Pentecost, and the festivals of Saints Peter and Paul. No copy of the first edition of Book I is known to survive, though its entry at Stationers' Hall has been traced and found to have been recorded there under date of January 10th, 1605, published by Thomas East.[1] The full title-page of the second edition of this work is:

Gradualia | *Ac* | *Cantiones Sac* | *rae, quinis, quaternis trinisque* | *vocibus concinnatæ.* | *Lib. Primus.* | Authore Gulielmo Byrde, Organista | Regio Anglo. | Editio Secunda, priore emendatior. | Dulcia defecta modulatur carmina linguâ | Cantator Cygnus funeris ipse sui. Martialis. | Londoni, | Excudebat H. L. Impensis Ricardi Redmeri, | Stella aurea in D. Pauli Cœmeterio.— 1610. (Graduals and Sacred Songs, arranged for 5, 4, and 3 voices. Book I. By William Byrd, Organist to the King, Englishman. Second edition, revised. The Swan, a singer with a

[1] Dr. Fellowes gives this information. Sir Richard Terry retains 1607 on the title page of those motets which he has edited for the Carnegie Trust. But Mr Barclay Squire now accepts 1605 in place of 1607 which he gives in the second edition of Grove's *Dictionary*.

failing tongue, utters sweet songs of his own demise (Martial). Printed in London by H. L. at the charge of Richard Redmire, the Golden Star, St. Paul's Churchyard 1610.)

The strain of melancholy which makes him talk of swan-songs in the title and dedication of this book is a trait of Byrd's character which shows itself as pathos in his music. In the introduction to the second book he speaks of the death of some of his distinguished pupils (viris sane ea arte egregie peritis). This may have saddened him, though in the same place he speaks of the work as an offering of gratitude for the divine goodness to him. It is quite likely too that the state of public opinion had become embittered once more towards Roman Catholicism after the failure of the Gunpowder Plot, just as it had done nearly twenty years earlier after the failure of the invasion of the Armada when Byrd published his *Cantiones Sacrae*. Be that as it may, Byrd's genius lent itself, in spite of his great powers of expressing joy, to charging grave music like *Ave Verum Corpus* with pathos ; the phrase ' miserere mei' in this motet, sung by tenor and alto in thirds and afterwards repeated by every part in imitation, is abject. This is one of the most frequently performed works of Byrd, and it can be obtained on the gramophone (H.M.V. E305).[1] It is an

---

[1] N.B.—There is a cut in this record, by which fourteen bars are omitted before the Amen. These are a repetition of what has previously been heard, so that the mutilation is not very serious.

example, though not perhaps the most striking, of a quality that is compounded of austerity, sobriety, and seriousness with just a touch of sadness, that we shall call his gravity. Three of the four voice parts are low pitched, and they move slowly and fairly homophonically, producing a subdued effect. To the modern listener homophonic music inevitably sounds like so much harmony; the harmony of *Ave Verum Corpus* he will notice sounds queer; the reason for this is the repeated juxtaposition of the chords of D major and F major. The motet is in G minor (taking the liberty for convenience sake to assign keys to this modal and transitional music); the chord of D major is the dominant of the key, while D minor has F as its relative major. The two chords are therefore quite nearly related— brothers-in-law in fact, but like brothers-in-law they differ profoundly in temperament. When therefore Byrd begins

he plunges the ear into an unstable world in which the ground, as it were, dissolves beneath it and leaves the poor bewildered organ to ask: ' Are you talking flats or sharps ?—you can't talk both at once, you know.' Byrd and his contemporaries, however, did sometimes do something which is

very much like that. They certainly made no
bones about having an F sharp in one part
followed immediately by an F natural in another
(this is called 'false relation'). Here the effect
is peculiarly strong because the false relation is
between the outside parts. And later in the
motet he aggravates the offence by employing
the chord of C along with the chord of F, which
makes the whole progression shout F major against
the last word of the previous phrase which was an
unrepentant D major. Shouting, however, is a
bad metaphor, for the effect is rather one of
crushing by quietness, though it is only the effect
of three centuries of harmony which raises this
antagonism. To Byrd, as to us if we can disabuse
our mind of its modern harmonic preoccupations,
it spelt a spacious dissolving effect which well
expresses the mystery of the True Body. But we
may find greater difficulty in reconciling ourselves
to the ugly juxtaposition of the chords of D major
and C major each in root position, that occurs in
Responsum accepit Simeon (Simeon received the
reply) No. 5 Bk. I. We find too that a number of
these motets which are short and straightforward
have little more than a ceremonial value, like much
of the dignified but otherwise not specially
distinguished music that has been written by a
long line of composers of varying ability for the
service of the English Church. *Benedicta et
Venerabilis* (No. 7 in this book) is of this type.
So too is *Alleluia Ave Maria* (No. 20) for

73

Septuagesima, in which a text compounded of fragments of Scripture and enunciation of doctrine makes dull music. On the other hand where the doctrine appeals to Byrd's mysticism, such as the Incarnation in *Ave Verum Corpus*, we get very profound feeling often conveyed in strong harmonic progressions. An example of a sacred mystery being so expressed is *Post Partum Virgo* (No. 18) where at the words ' inviolata permansisti ' (Thou hast born a child yet remained a virgin inviolate) Byrd proceeds from his home key of D minor by means of a B natural towards A minor with a G natural until he reaches the end of his phrase, where he sharpens it and dissolves into A major. Among other five-part motets of this book *Rorate Cæli*[1] (No. 13) (Rain dew from above, O ye heavens) shows traces of the austerity which Byrd could mingle with his most splendid and vigorous conceptions. It is constructed in the same form as the aria of later times : there is a middle section for three solo voices, completed by a Gloria for all five parts, but at the end in spite of finishing on the tonic there is a direction to repeat the first part. *Justorum Animæ* (The souls of the Righteous) (No. 31) is one of the better known Latin motets of Byrd : it is smoother than many of his works but has not the sensuous quality of the Italian masters—always in Byrd is the touch of austerity which belongs to our race and climate. Of the four-part motets in this

[1] Published separately by the Oxford University Press.

volume noteworthy numbers beside *Ave Verum Corpus* are Nos. 3, 10, 15 and 20. No. 3 *Sacerdotes Domini* (The Priests of the Lord) is simple and conceived somewhat homophonically —nothing like the chorales of Bach of course, but sufficiently to make the surging Alleluias at the end stronger by contrast.[1] No. 10 is in two parts and is noteworthy in several respects. The tenor enunciates the words ' Christus resurgens ' (Christ rising from the dead) to a plain song melody ; the other voices enter immediately after with the words ' ex mortuis jam non moritur ' (now no longer dieth) while the tenor continues to sing over and over again the same plain-song as a semibreve *canto fermo* though with different words. The words of the second part are non-scriptural and by their challenging tone add to the general feeling of excitement which the very wide compass of the voices (low E for bass and high F for treble) creates : Dicant nunc Judæi quomodo milites custodientes sepulchrum perdiderunt regem ad lapidis positionem. Quare non servabant petram justitiæ ? Aut sepultum reddant aut resurgentem adorent, nobiscum dicentes, Alleluia. (Let the Jews now tell how the soldiers who guarded the tomb have lost a king while the stone was in its place. Why did they not keep safe the rock of Justice ? Either let them restore him who was buried or let them worship him who

[1] Published separately by the Oxford University Press.

is risen and join with us in our Alleluias.) No. 15, *In manus tuas commendo meum spiritum* (Into Thy hands I commend my spirit) is confident and quietly happy, an effect which Byrd obtains by the use of little figures which thread in and out of the parts. No. 20, *Deo Gratias*, is a short grace, simple, charming and reverent. Of the three-part motets No. 8, *Angelus Domini descendit* for two sopranos and tenor is short, has a similar religious charm, goes to both sides of the key (A major and C minor from the prevailing tonality of F major), but is most interesting as showing the way in which the words, by that mysterious power of which Byrd speaks in his preface, create musical phrases of the right shape to express them. No. 10 is one of the earliest pieces of Passion Music extant and superficially has not much resemblance to the great form of art brought to perfection 150 years later by Bach. *Turbarum Voces in Passione Domini Nostri secundum Joannem*[1] (The Voices of the Crowds in the Passion of our Lord according to St. John) is its full title and it consists of fourteen short interjectory choruses representing the answers of the crowd to Pilate, the various sayings of the Jews, the priests and the soldiers. The narrative portions are not set to music, neither are the words of Jesus and the other characters treated in the semi-dramatic manner of later times. The priest

[1] Edited by W. Barclay Squire, and published separately by Novello.

read the scriptural story, leaving to the choir only these crowd utterances. The choruses in the Bach *Passions* are of two kinds: the reflective utterances of the worshipper and the dramatically conceived interjections of the crowd at the trial and crucifixion. So that the rudimentary dramatisation of the Passion story which began with a treatment like Byrd's of the crowd choruses, though it developed into the special oratorio form employed by Bach, yet retained to the end this dramatic treatment of the chorus. Byrd's music is very simple, homophonic to represent the discipline of the priestly party and the spokesmen of the people who produce their legal arguments with one mind and one voice, contrapuntal with entries in imitation to represent the greater excitement of the mob when they cry ' Not this man ' or ' Crucify'.

The title of the second book of *Gradualia,* published in 1607 ran: *Gradualia: | Seu Cantionum Sacrarum | Quarum aliæ ad Quatuor, | aliæ verò ad | Quinque et Sex voces editæ sunt. | Liber Secundus. |* Authore Gulielmo Byrde Organista | Regio, Anglo. | Musica Divinos profert modulamine Cantus : Iubilum in Ore, favum in Corde, et in Aure melos. | Excudebat Thomas Este Londini, ex assignatione | Gulielmi Barley 1607. (Graduals or Sacred Songs: Of which some are written for four but others for five and six voices. Book II. By William Byrd, organist to the King, Englishman. Music brings forward divine songs in its measures : a cry of joy upon the lips, a sweetness in the heart, and to the ear a melody. Printed by Thomas East of London, at the assignation of William Barley. 1607.)

We may note about these title pages in passing that between 1607, when the second book was first published, and 1610, when the first book came out in a second edition, Thomas East's long partnership with Byrd had come to an end. We may observe also how persistently " Anglo " appears in all these Latin title pages, perhaps to make it clear that they were not importations from Italy. Coming to the music of the second book with its motets for the great festivals of the ecclesiastical year, we may compare *Hodie Christus natus est* in four parts with the madrigal *This Day Christ was born* in the 1611 set. It is impossible to know whether the first published was also the first composed, but in this case at any rate the English is a finer work than the Latin. The mood of the motet is more sober than that of the " caroll " ; the four parts keep close together, and there is no high writing for soprano voices like that which gives such elation to the six-part madrigal. There is, however, a similar change to triple rhythm at the *Alleluias* in both. Elsewhere (in *This Sweet and Merry Month*, for example) Byrd preserves identical rhythmic treatment in two settings of the same words. The opening of No. 18 *O quam suavis* (O how pleasant is Thy

Spirit, O Lord) is highly coloured and may be quoted

A striking number among the Easter motets is *Victimæ Paschali* (Unto Christ the Victim) in which at the words 'Mors et Vita duello conflixere mirando' (Death and Life strove in a wondrous duel) an extraordinary piece of two-part writing between alto and tenor—a very vigorous duel—leads to a gorgeous climax at the triumph of Life. *Psallite Domino* No. 29 which belongs to Ascensiontide, is interesting in that it shows how expressive simple ascending and descending scales can be made. In *Veni, Veni Sancte Spiritus* No. 36 (Come Holy Spirit) for Pentecost the counterpoint is smooth and closely wrought like the best work of the Italian masters; there is a picturesque modulation to a cadence in E major at the words 'dulce refrigerium' (sweet consolation) and the words 'flecte quod rigidum' (bend what is stiff) are suggestively treated in six short bars; the Amens, as in many of these late elaborate motets, move in parallel thirds and sixths between changing parts. A similar feature is found in the next motet No. 37, *Non relinquam orphanos* (I will not leave you comfortless[1])—a fine number in which Alleluias set to phrases of bold outline keep breaking in upon the words of the text. Among the six-part motets for the feast of St. Peter is one with the words : Tu es pastor ovium, princeps Apostolorum, tibi traditæ sunt claves regni cœlorum (Thou art the shepherd of the sheep, chiefest of the Apostles, and to thee are delivered the keys of the kingdom of heaven). The title *princeps Apostolorum* had a papistical sound in those days which was too much for the printer's courage ; only the first four words are printed. Words are also missing from No. 40, *Solve jubente Deo*, and No. 42, *Hodie Simon Petrus.*

The *Alleluias* are a great feature of the *Gradualia.* In them Byrd shows an apparently inexhaustible resource, just as he does in varying the cadence formulæ of his madrigals and of his *Amens* in the English Church music. Moreover they seem to be a kind of epilogue embodying the feeling of the preceding words in the same sort of way as the aria in a later phase of vocal music embodies and elaborates the emotions evoked by the incidents of the preceding recitative. The proportions, of course, are reversed, but there would seem to be no other explanation to account for the fertility of invention and profound beauty of the music set to words which have in themselves none of the force on which Byrd, according to his own profession, relied for his inspiration.

[1] Published under this title by Novello, edited by John E. West, price 4d.

An innovation in motet writing is found in the first book of *Gradualia,* which may have been due to the lack of opportunity for using these motets in their proper setting of the Mass. Some have words assigned to two vocal parts only, the remaining parts being given to viols. This certainly looks as though Byrd must have had in mind performances of these works under conditions similar to the singing of madrigals at private parties. We know that there were occasional clandestine celebrations of the Mass in private chapels such as that described by Father Weston[1] who tells of the week's festival at the house of Mr Bold in these words: " they had a chapel . . . an organ likewise and other musical instruments, and moreover singers of both sexes belonging to the family. . . . Thus during the course of these days we celebrated, as it were, a long octave of some magnificent festival ".[2] But this shows how rare such ecclesiastical performances were. At private musical parties it was customary, as we have seen, to use the viols either as an alternative or as a supplement to the voices, and Byrd here applies to the singing of motets a plan which he had tried by successful experiment in his 1589 set of madrigals.

[1] See below, p. 197.

[2] *The Troubles of our Catholic Forefathers.* II p. 142. The original letter in which this passage occurs is dated June 30th, 1601, and is preserved at Stonyhurst.

There are also one or two things which do not come into the categories we have discussed : thus, there, is a compline hymn, *Christe qui lux es et dies*[1] (O Christ who art the light and day), founded on a plain song, which is first enunciated in unison and then given in five-part harmony with the melody allotted to each part in turn in the five succeeding verses. It is very pleasing and simple and—being unlike anything that has been touched by classical influences—when heard in a cathedral sounds refreshingly remote from the world and the present.

Among the unpublished music are settings of the Lamentations, and among the canons already mentioned are nineteen based on the plain song *Miserere*. Thomas Morley in his famous *Plaine and Easie Introduction to Practicall Musicke* (1597) refers to a competition between Byrd and the elder Ferrabosco, which recalls the periodical exchange of manuscripts between Brahms and Joachim. Byrd and his antagonist, however, took the same text—*Miserere*, and published their results in 1603 in a book entitled *Medulla*[2] *Musicke. Sucked out of the sappe of Two of the most famous Musitians that euer were in this land, namely Master William Byrd . . . and Master Alfonso Ferabosco . . . either of whom having made* 40^tie *severall waies (without*

---

[1] Published by the Oxford University Press, and recently (1927) recorded for the gramophone in York Minster (H.M.V. C1334).

[2] Medulla—Latin for marrow.

contention) *showing most rare and intricate skill in* 2 *partes in one vpon the playne songe* " Miserere." There is no copy extant. We close this chapter with Morley's own description of this competition, to show both the charm of Morley's writing and to throw a sidelight on the character of Byrd. (Morley, *Plaine and Easie Introduction*, Pt. II, first edn., p. 115) :

' But if you thinke to imploy anie time in making of those, I would counsell you diligentlie to peruse those waies which my louing Maister (neuer without reuerence to be named of the musicians) M. *Bird*, and M. *Alphonso* in a vertuous contention in loue betwixt themselves, made upon the plainsong of *Miserere*, but a contention, as I saide, in loue : which caused them striue euery one to surmount another, without malice, enuie or backbiting : but by great labour, studie, and paines, ech making other censure of that which they had done. Which contention of theirs (specially without enuie) caused them both become excellent in that kind, and winne such a name, and gaine such credite, as will neuer perish so long as Musicke indureth. Therefore, there is no waie readier to cause you become perfect, than to contend with some one or other, not in malice (for so is your contention uppon passion, not for loue of vertue) but in loue shewing your adversarie your worke, and not skorning to bee corrected of him, and to amende your fault if hee speake with reason : but of this enough. To return to M. *Bird*, and M. *Alphonso*, though either of them made to the number of fortie waies and could haue made infinite more at

83

their pleasure, yet hath one manne, my friend and fellow
M. *George Waterhouse*, vpon the same plainsong of
Miserere, for varietie surpassed all who euer laboured
in that kinde of studie. For, hee hath alreadie made a
thousand waies (yea and though I should talke of halfe
as manie more, I should not be farre wide of the truth)
euery one different and seuerall from another.'

CHAPTER IV

THE Latin Church music was written as unaccompanied vocal music. There were organs, however, in English cathedrals long before the sixteenth century. There is a vivid, almost alarming, account of an organ erected in Winchester Cathedral before 951 which had 400 pipes and was blown by seventy strong men. There were ten pipes to each note, sounding probably octaves and fifths, which made a noise ' like thunder ' so that ' the hearers stopped their ears with their hands and were unable to draw near or bear the sound '. It obviously impressed the monk who has left us this description of it, but the improved instruments of later centuries were doubtless less terrifying in their effect and were used for supporting the voices. They did not play an independent part, but when used at all doubled the voice parts. That this was done appears from the existence of organ books. It is out of the question that organ accompaniment was introduced with the English liturgy. The English Cathedrals were compelled to obtain new music for the new services : a system of circulating new music was already in vogue ; all of Byrd's working life came during a period when Protestantism prevailed and Latin music was no longer required for the cathedral services. He therefore published his motets for the use of such private persons as cared to buy them, but circulated his new liturgical music in the usual way. And so we find scattered through the country in cathedral libraries organ parts which were copied in short score into the organist's book at the same time as the separate voice parts were copied into the choristers' books. These organ parts were not merely 'short' but abbreviated scores in which the inner parts were only sketched, and in the case of compositions for five or six voices not more than four parts were set out simultaneously. For example there is in the library of Christ Church, Oxford, an organ part of the third service, which it calls ' Mr. Bird's three minnoms ', in which three of the five parts are written out in the first bar only ; thereafter through the whole of the *Magnificat* and *Nunc Dimittis* (there are no morning canticles belonging to this setting) only the top and bottom parts appear. The few of these organ books which survive have been found useful by editors when scoring Byrd's services from the part books for modern publication, and in the big quarto edition of the Carnegie collection of Tudor church music these organ parts are exactly reproduced; in the octavo edition for practical use by singers the published organ part is merely a reduction of the vocal score and contains the full harmony. All of Byrd's four services are provided with organ accompaniments, and in one of them (known as the Second Service) Byrd makes an innovation that has been followed by writers for the Anglican liturgy ever since. Both *Magnificat* and *Nunc Dimittis* open with a short prelude for organ alone (the same prelude for both), upon which is superimposed the first words of the canticle by a solo alto, then the full choir enters but is interrupted by a solo ' verse '. A tenor sings ' He hath put down ', and a treble chants ' As he promised ' to the old plain-song Tonus Peregrinus. In the *Nunc Dimittis* four sopranos and altos sing the verse ' To be a light '—an arrangement which enhances the meaning of the words. The organ part is a true accompaniment and often goes above the solo voice with good effect. This service was printed by Barnard, who made and published a printed collection of Church music in 1641, and is called by him *Mr. W. Bird's second Service with verses to the Organ.* This new method of ecclesiastical composition was also used by Byrd in a number of anthems, and his younger contemporaries, Weelkes and Gibbons, followed him in this innovation of writing solo ' verses '.

The two services already mentioned are both ' short ' services, but what is known as *the* Short Service is Byrd in D minor (transposed to F minor for present use), which is a setting of the morning as well as the evening canticles. Besides these three ' short ' services and a fourth in F of which only fragments are at present known, Byrd wrote a ' great ' service. ' Short ' and Great ' are semi-technical descriptions of two opposite ways of setting words. The story of the attack of the Council of Trent upon musicians for the excessive elaboration and other undesirable features of their settings of the Mass, and of the acceptance of Palestrina's *Missa Papæ Marcelli* as a model, is well known. The council of Trent itself, which assembled in 1543 to deal with more serious problems than the chanting of the liturgy, did finally turn to purging the Roman service of many abuses. But it was too late to stave off the Protestant secession, and in England even more than in Luther's own Germany, reformers had long before 1563 gone into details with church composers as to what they might and might not do. Archbishop Cranmer had, as we have seen, asserted the principle of one syllable to a note in 1544, and the ' short ' services are the result of obedience to the spirit of that recommendation. Composers however could hardly be expected to renounce all their technical skill, nor to chain the flight of their imaginations by restrictions so serious as a rigid adherence to the clear and rapid recitation of the words. Music has a way of demanding a large measure of autonomy and insisting on developing according to its own laws. To a point it will adapt itself to drama or words or dance if these other arts will meet it half way.

But a musical phrase is lamed if its course is determined for it entirely by verbal and not at all by musical considerations. Composers therefore provided plain and straightforward services for ordinary use, but reserved to themselves the pleasure of giving full rein to their inspiration in more spacious works which would be suitable for liturgical performance on high festivals. Such a work is Byrd's ' Great ' service.

Byrd in D minor is an unadorned setting, very direct and homophonic in style. Though its music is an admirable vehicle for the words—the ' underlaying ' of words was one of Byrd's most notable qualities—its general musical effect is quite frankly dull. The range of harmonic combinations and progressions at the disposal of a composer of this period was limited, and the modern ear can only hear note against note counterpoint (' first species ' is the pundits' name for this) as blocks of harmony. The alternation of major and minor sounds aimless and confused (which it certainly is not), and it was this effect which led later composers to avoid, and theorists to prohibit, false relations. Byrd was more concerned with drawing the melody of each part than with chord progressions. In other words, he wrote them as counterpoint, we hear them as harmony. The *Te Deum* ends with a very effective use of the major and minor third simultaneously. It happens to occur on the word ' confounded ' but slips off on to the smoothest concord, so that the idea of the word and the escape from what it signifies are prettily suggested, though Byrd may have thought of it only as so much part-writing. The *Magnificat* is recorded for gramophone (H.M.V. E291), and a good idea can be obtained from the record of the rhythmic freedom with which this music should be sung. The *Nunc Dimittis* is constructed upon the rhythmic plan of having each phrase (after the first) anticipated a beat by the treble. This service has been in continual use since Byrd's own day, and together with the anthems *Bow Thine Ear* and *Sing Joyfully* has kept his name in remembrance during the long period when the rest of his work was practically forgotten. His reputation was remembered all through the seventeenth and eighteenth centuries, but his style was out of favour and his music with these exceptions praised but unperformed. The reason for the preservation of these few pieces in the repertoire is that they were included by Barnard in his collection of 1641 and in the later collection of Boyce. Barnard was a minor canon of St Paul's in the time of Charles I. On his title page he writes *The First Book of Selected Church Musick consisting of Services and Anthems such as are now used in the Cathedrall and Collegiat Churches of this Kingdome.* 'Never before printed. Whereby such Bookes as were heretofore with much difficulty and charges transcribed for the use of the Quire, are now to the saving of much labour and expense, publisht for the general good of all such as shall desire them either for publick or private exercise. Collected out of divers approved authors.' The greater convenience of printed books undermined the old circulating system and had the unforeseen result of limiting the repertoire to what the ready-made collection contained. As in other spheres of life the minimum became the maximum. A good many of the old manuscript part-books perished at the hands of Puritan iconoclasts, and Boyce's eighteenth-century selection (1760-78) replaced Barnard's three services and seven anthems with one service and three anthems. And so Byrd's reputation survived on this reduced representation except for occasional abortive revivals (such as that which produced Mr. Horsley's edition in the 'forties of last century), until the great revival of interest in him of the last quarter of a century.

The Great Service is a recent discovery. It seems likely that from Byrd's own day until May 1924 it was never sung. The latest date when it might have been performed would be in the sixteen-forties, when the publication of Barnard's book of services and the outbreak of the Civil War combined to remove it out of the current of tradition. Its recovery makes quite a romantic story, and must have given to Dr. Fellowes one of those breathless moments such as only fall to explorers and scholars. In the programme supplied to the audience at the first London performance he relates how he lighted on a masterpiece. He was working on the church music of Orlando Gibbons in Durham Cathedral when he found in the part-books an unknown service of Byrd. Two of the part-books were missing, but the required bass part was found in another set of books at Durham and part of the missing alto at Cambridge ; a few fragments were found in the British Museum and hints obtained from three organ books. With these texts Dr. Fellowes has been able to score and edit the complete work.

The first complete performance after an interval of nearly 300 years took place in Newcastle Cathedral on May 31st, 1924, when it was sung by the Newcastle Bach Choir under Dr W. G. Whittaker. The same choir in November of the same year gave three performances in London at St Margaret's, Westminster, and it has since been sung in York Minster and other churches. The evening service had been sung even earlier at St Michael's College, Tenbury, the foundation of Sir F. Gore Ouseley, which exists to cultivate church music and which is rich in Tudor part books and MSS. The College claims that its performance of the evening service on May 22nd, 1923, is the first since the early seventeenth century.

Under these circumstances it is perhaps permissible to examine the work in some detail and to compare it with the Masses where the Roman and Anglican rituals employ the same words.   It is laid out for two choirs of five voices each, but there is only a little ten-part writing, and the choirs are for the most part used antiphonally.   It consists of seven numbers, which belong to three distinct offices : the *Venite*, *Te Deum* and *Benedictus* to Matins, the *Kyrie* and *Creed* to the Communion, and the *Magnificat* and *Nunc Dimittis* to Evensong.   It has not therefore the unity which enables settings of the Mass which are too big for liturgical use (like Bach's B minor or Beethoven's Mass in D) to be given in concert performance, while on the other hand it has one unifying characteristic which is so devastating in effect as in itself to preclude continuous performance of the whole ; this is its key.   It is almost bare of modulations and the tonality of E flat[1] is made the more prominent by the persistent use of the tonic chord and by the continual soaring to the high tonic by treble and tenor.   Bach in the B minor Mass keeps the key of B minor for the most impressive moments (it was undoubtedly his favourite key, as C minor seems—though less markedly—to have been Beethoven's) and goes for the rest to all the related sharp keys and in one number (but only one), the *Agnus Dei*, goes to the flat key of G minor.   To hear Byrd's Service straight through as one hears Bach's Mass would be maddening, and when it was sung in London great care was taken not only to give it in an appropriate semi-liturgical form, but

[1] The original pitch is C.

93

broken up by voluntaries, lessons and addresses. Notwithstanding it is very much to be hoped that choral societies will take up the Great Service and perform it suitably interspersed with anthems, motets, and solos. For that it contains a wealth of fine music we may now see in detail.

The *Venite* is a straightforward movement, very like a short service in its treatment of the words; phrases like ' and ever shall be ' are repeated several times for the sake of musical effect, but there is no elaboration of phrase on single syllables except that some part may stand still for a moment on an unimportant word like a preposition or conjunction while the other parts have a little phrase in different rhythm. The *Te Deum* is naturally more elaborate and grows in complexity towards the end, though even here the only word to which Byrd assigns a little melismatic phrase is ' ever ' in ' lift them up for ever' and 'confounded ' at the end. This word he repeats over and over again and works up with quaver movement to a great pinacle of sound on the fresh-sounding chord of G. The *Benedictus* similarly works up to a tremendous climax of vigour and movement to the words ' world without end '. In this as in the previous movements considerable contrast is obtained by the alternate use of ' verse ' (i.e. sung by solo voice) and full choir, the effect being enhanced by the omission of the bass from the ' verse ' sections. The only words with which melodic play is made (until the end) are ' hate '

and ' enemies '.   The *Kyrie* is a very tender little
movement with a little rising phrase used in
imitation for the word ' beseech ', which imparts a
touch of urgency to the prayer.   The setting of
the Creed may be compared with the *Credo*
sections of the Latin Masses, and shows that there
is a difference in style.   Byrd seems to have
realised in setting English that he would best
' frame to the life of the words ' his melodies if
he kept them closer to natural speech rhythm
than in Latin.   And so there are no melismatic
passages to the word ' heaven ' (which indeed he
treats as a single syllable), nor are there many
touches of musical word painting.   'Descended'
is not illustrated, though there is a fine springing
phrase in the bass to the words ' ascended into
heaven ' which is used in a modified shape in the
other parts.   The most striking effects of this
kind are an insistence on the chord of D flat all
through the section describing the passion, and a
daring suggestion of chattering at the words ' who
spake by the Prophets '.   On the whole the
English words seem to call out a blunter kind of
treatment, and the melodic outline of the Great
Service is much more rugged than that of the
Masses, which are nearer to the smooth phrases
of Palestrina.

The *Magnificat* is undoubtedly the most
splendid number in the whole service and is sung
throughout by a full choir.   One of the few
extended melismatic passages occurs on the word

95

' his ' in ' He hath shewed strength with his arm '. The scattering of the proud is done with a dotted-note figure of some violence. There is a pictorial suggestiveness about the descending scale passage to which the words ' throughout all generations ' are set, while in ' his seed for ever ' each part sings the same notes (though of course at different pitches) one after the other in overlapping phrases which picture an endless chain. The *Gloria* contains one of those passages that sound like pealing bells of which Byrd so frequently makes use when he wishes to express joy. The *Nunc Dimittis* is chiefly noteworthy for the magnificent *Gloria* which brings the work to a conclusion. This has been recorded for gramophone (H.M.V. E291). It begins with a short phrase of almost unanimous homophony, but very soon sets the voice upon independent paths, spacing them out more and more upon their own tracks, yet at the same time binding them into a different relationship with one another, namely that of imitation, until by the time ' world without end ' is reached the mounting phrases form a kind of angelic escalator of sound rising to Heaven. These words, it should be noticed, are set to a phrase of very long notes in the bass part which appears meanwhile in the other parts in shorter imitations and variants. The first bars of this *Gloria* may be commended to those who have a technical interest in harmony, as they show concisely the point reached by Byrd on the way to the diatonic harmony on which Bach and Handel built, and which has been the foundation of all subsequent music until the 'new' music of the last thirty years. In his first cadence he sits down quite definitely though only for a brief moment in the key of C major,[1] but quickly turns back by changing it to C minor.[2] This cadence is one of the permitted modulations in the Ionian mode, and 'modulation' in music of this period means a point of rest, not a shifting of the balance of tonality. None the less to the ear it only differs from a modern modulation in that the harmony begins to turn back again towards the flat keys instead of going on somewhere else. It has no sooner touched the chord of E flat once more than a suspended B flat over a chord of F major resolves on to an A natural and is apparently going to pitchfork us into the key of B flat. A classical composer could not have avoided treating this as a dominant chord and modulating with or without decoration or interruption into B flat major, while a modern composer could only have escaped doing the same thing by treating it as an intermediate progression between more widely separated harmonies. Byrd does neither ; he calmly takes it straight back on to the chord of E flat. It is

[1] The same cadence occurs in the *Magnificat* at 'the imagination of their hearts.'

[2] In the quarto edition of Tudor Church Music the original pitch is kept ; for purposes of performance the octavo edition is issued in a transposed version a minor third higher.

97

this kind of writing which sounds strange to the ear attuned to classical music. The logic of it is not of course harmonic at all—it is of doubtful legitimacy to talk of keys—but contrapuntal. The A natural in the soprano part happens melodically and is not meant, as it would be in later music, to be a catchpoint leading into another tonal track. In the space of a few bars we therefore see how far Byrd had got on the road to classical harmony and how far music still had to go. Some of Byrd's more striking harmonic usages will be observed in this way. The Great Service is not remarkable from this point of view. Rather it is remarkable for the great sweep, vitality and splendour of the whole design (the cumulative effect of the separate numbers is a proof that the three series were conceived as one great design), achieved with exceptional directness of expression yet with none of the sternness of Taverner or Tallis and with less of the harshness that Byrd himself uses boldly elsewhere. Great variety of tone and expression is made possible by the use of two choirs used antiphonally and together, and by the use of ' verses ' for groups of solo voices—resources of which he does not avail himself in his settings of the Mass—and by the grouping of the voices to produce variety of tone colour as in the five-part Mass.

Beside these ambitious and inspiring works to be written for the new English liturgy there

were needed also musical settings for the humbler
(from a musical point of view) parts of the service,
the Preces, the Responses, the Psalms and the
Litany. For all of these Byrd produced suitable
music, probably in his youth and very possibly
before he left Lincoln. He set the Preces three
times (i.e., the short prayers recited by the
priest and answered by the congregation between
the Absolution and the Venite), the longer set of
Preces and Responses that come after the Creed
once, and the Litany once. Attached to the
Preces are certain selected Psalms, or rather
portions of Psalms, set to a kind of free chant.
These are described in the MSS. and in Barnard's
book as ' Mr. Byrd's First (or Second) Preces and
Psalms ', and the Psalms are always attached by
their title to the foregoing Preces. It seems
likely that the Psalms of the day were not sung
except on special occasions, and some colour is
lent to this view by the fact that one of these
' Psalms to Mr. Byrd's Second Preces ' is the
special Psalm for Ascension Day, *Lift up your
heads*. But exactly why these Preces and these
few specially treated verses of Psalms are so
closely connected is not known. The tradition
which takes this connection for granted has been
broken, and in liturgical matters tradition
explains more than many printed forms of service.
It had been customary in the old Latin usage to
sing psalms on special occasions, but there are
no settings by English composers for the Latin

99

service, but the practice plainly was continued in the reformed service to English words, at any rate at festivals. At other times the Psalms would be recited. There is one further point of interest about these Psalms and that is that the Third Psalm to the Second Preces, *Teach me O Lord*, has solo verses with organ accompaniment alternating with the full choir. As we have already seen, Byrd wrote a 'verse' service and he also wrote 'verse' anthems; this Psalm, possibly earlier in date than the others, may mark the point of divergence from tradition. If the priest and congregation (or choir) were in the habit of reciting alternative verses of the Psalms it is not a very big step to assigning alternate verses to solo voice and chorus. The experiment once made in this form could then be applied also to other parts of the service and to anthems, where it was greatly developed by Gibbons. In the time of Purcell under the French influence of the period these solos almost overshadowed the choral part.

Many of Byrd's English anthems have been preserved only in manuscript part-books in various cathedral and collegiate libraries, and are now being printed by the Carnegie Trustees for the first time. Barnard and Boyce in earlier times printed their small selection, and a number of compositions which are entitled to the description of anthems were printed by Byrd himself in the three sets of madrigals which he published in

1588, 1589 and 1611. In each of these collections he included settings of the psalms or portions of psalms which may be appropriately used in church as anthems. But as these collections were made for domestic use, and Byrd's avowed purpose in including 'some solemn' among 'others joyful' was to provide madrigal parties with songs of every mood, they must not be regarded as church music but are better considered in relation to the music of the home, which is so important and so distinctive a feature of the Elizabethan period. For liturgical purpose Byrd wrote four anthems which he contributed to a collection made by Sir William Leighton called *Teares or Lamentacions of a Sorrowful Soule*. This volume, which was published in 1614, included two anthems by Orlando Gibbons.

Bow Thine Ear and *Sing Joyfully*, the two anthems which owing to their inclusion in Boyce's Cathedral Music have never been entirely forgotten, do fairly represent Byrd's style in two characteristic moods—the solemn and the joyful. *Bow Thine Ear* is an extremely sad work and Byrd even in his solemn vein does not always strike a note of such desolation, but it shows his characteristic gravity, as *Sing Joyfully* shows his vigour. In the latter the orchestral effects at ' Bring forth the pleasant harp and the viol ; blow the trumpet ' cannot fail to attract attention. *Bow Thine Ear* is an adaptation to English words of the second part of the motet

Ne irascaris (O Lord turn thy wrath) which belongs to the 1589 volume of *Cantiones Sacrae*. The feeling of desertion and desolation gradually wraps one round as the anthem proceeds, and the words ' Jerusalem is wasted quite ' are set to a pathetic little fragment of melody which is reiterated in imitation as the soul confronts its own despair. A good example of Byrd's use of voices in a manner akin to an organist's use of his stops occurs in the passage immediately preceding, when the four upper voices sing in the middle of their register ' Thy Sion is wasted and brought low ' to be followed at once by the four lower voices singing it in their lower registers. This ' registering ' of the voices produces an effect of colour vivid enough to satisfy even the modern passion for bright orchestral hues and sharp contrasts.

Some other anthems of a solemn nature or expressive of a humble frame of mind are noteworthy in various ways. In *O God, whom our offences have displeased*, Byrd makes frequent use of a little ornamental figure on important words like ' beseech ' very much in the manner of the ornaments which he wrote in his virginal music, and to get the same sort of emphasis as Beethoven would have done by a sforzando. *O Lord rebuke me not* is an anthem ' with verses to the organ ', in which the chorus echoes what the soloist has just sung, thus expressing both a personal and a corporate penitence. Harmonically this anthem shows an advance towards more modern methods. Its tonality is F major, but he starts the last verse definitely in the key of G major; he has prepared the way to this by making an orthodox cadence on to a chord of D major. But the new key (it is a key and does not sound in the least modal) gives a new direction to the music with a remarkably fresh effect at the words 'Turn Thee, O Lord.' In quite a modern way the tonality shifts into D major and then back into the flats via A minor. *Alack, when I look back* is a true penitential anthem in which a solo voice (alto) and a five-part chorus alternate as in *O Lord, rebuke me not*. Its words are not biblical but come from the *Paradise of Dainty Devises* (1578) and are worth quoting :

Alacke when I looke backe, upon my youth thatz paste,
And deepely ponder youthes offence, and youths reward at
    laste
With sighes and teares I saie, O God, I not denie,
My youth with follie hath deserved, with follie for to die.
But yet if ever synfull man, might mercie move to ruthe,
Good Lorde with mercie doe forgive, the follies of my youthe.

In youth I rangde the feelds, where vices all did growe
In youth alas I wanted grace, such vise to ouerthrowe,
In youth what I thought sweete, moste bitter now do finde,
Thus hath the follies of my youth, with folly kept me blind
Yet as the Egle[1] casts her bill, whereby her age renueth,
So Lorde with mercie doe forgive, the follies of my youth.
                     Mr. Hunnis.

[1] So the original poem ; in the anthem the bird is the eyass, or hawk.

In *How long shall mine enemies triumph over me ?* there is a little point which shows the working of that hidden power to shape melody which Byrd declared that words possessed. Five verses of the thirteenth psalm provide the text, of which four express a humble frame of mind, but in the fifth there is a sudden uprush of renewed confidence. Byrd at once takes his high parts, soprano and tenor, a tone higher than anything they have touched before, making the peak of the phrase occur on the syllable *joy* of *joyful*.

Beside *Sing joyfully* there is a very fine joyous anthem which is straightforward to sing and full of the splendid exaltation which Byrd achieved in his more florid and vigorous motets. Byrd's fondness for bells and the bell-like effects he introduces into his music to express exaltation have already been noted. In *O Praise the Lord, Ye Saints Above* the words ' The gladsome sound of silver bells, O praise Him with your ringing ' give him an opportunity to employ his favourite device, and in the corresponding couplet

> ' And virtuous wits do nothing else
> But laud him with your singing '

he turns some scale passages to brilliant effect. The whole anthem is full of magnificently melodious phrases which skilfully reproduce the rhythm of the words ; it begins boldly and ends exuberantly. The same kind of directness, but attached to different feelings, is to be found in

Prevent us O Lord, which does, however, contain several long melismatic passages in the inner parts ; in *O God give ear,* a short collect written in major tonality with orthodox classical leanings to dominant harmony in the middle, and laid out for six voices to produce the smooth rolling effect that suits the acoustic properties of cathedral churches ; and in *Arise O Lord,* which by its crispness provides a strong contrast to the vigour and florid writing of *Exsurge Domine.* There is a touch of anger in *O God the proud,* with its incisive rhythms and terrific earnestness on a grim melisma to the word ' anger ' in the second alto part. Prayers for the king's majesty strike a rather different note. *Thou God that guid'st both Heaven and Earth* was printed by Barnard ; it is a verse anthem and the organ part is unusually long and full, with quite a considerable little symphony of its own in the middle. The words of *Behold O God* are worth quoting :

Behold O God the sad and heavy case
   Wherein we stand as simple sheep forlorn,
If death possess whom life doth yet embrace,
   Then may we wail that we were ever born ;
Wherefore, good Lord, vouchsafe that we may sing,
   And praise thy Name for our most sacred king.

O Lord thou know'st that if the head but ache
   The body must partaker be of pain,
And every limb will tremble shake and quake
   Till health possess her wonted course again ;

Wherefore good Lord stir up our hearts to sing
 And praise thy Name for our most sacred king.

Behold also what bloody broils may rise
 Throughout the flock for want of such a one,
What slaughters great, what clamours and what cries
 With wringing hands, with tears and many a groan ;
This, Lord, prevent, and give us grace to sing,
 And Praise thy Name for our most sacred king.

We all confess our sins such plagues deserve,
 But yet, good Lord, thy mercy great extend,
And suffer not thy silly flock to starve,
 Beseeching thee thy gracious ears to bend ;
And still vouchsafe that we may always sing
 And praise thy Name for our most sacred king.

The four verses Byrd has set to two sections of music, but seems to have considered the first verse of each pair only when composing it, as the word-painting shows. 'Heavy' has an expressive chromatic note (A flat in G minor), while the imitations in the two voice parts and the organ give a realistic turn to 'tremble shake and quake'. It is noteworthy that this is a verse anthem for two voices in duet alternating with full choir in five parts. *O Lord make thy servant Elizabeth* is the most attractive to hear, as it has the smooth rolling effect of *O God give ear*. It was printed by Barnard with the name of the reigning king Charles, which led to a misapprehension whether it was originally a Latin motet.

The last works Byrd ever published were four contributions to Sir William Leighton's *Teares or Lamentacions of a Sorrowfull Soule*, which came out in 1614, and the names of Wilbye, Warde, Weelkes, Pilkington, Ford are found among the contributors. Coperario, Ferrabosco, Bull, and Orlando Gibbons also contributed a number of anthems to this volume. A selection of them was edited by Sir Frederick Bridge some years ago and republished in a collection of a dozen Elizabethan anthems, which have thus begun to find their way back into the Cathedral repertory. *Come, Come, Help O God* is a penitential anthem in which use is made of passages in which two parts sing together in minor thirds and tenths with a mournful effect, and in which the voices take turns in combining with one another but rarely sing all together. *Looke Downe O Lord* is clear and simple. There is a melismatic passage in imitation for the two top voices on the word 'joy', but Byrd seems to have liked the effect so much that he uses an abbreviated version of the same phrase again a few bars later on quite unimportant words, which is unusual with him. *I laid me down to rest* is tender and imaginative and there are two picturesque points. After a complete close on the chord of A major and a rest, a second verse to the words '*His angels pitcht me round about*' starts in block harmony which thus emphasises the new idea ; while a little later when the angels are described as ' Both coming in and going out, They guard me with security ' the movement of the parts is descriptive without being overdone. It ends quietly on an ordinary dominant cadence with a passing 7th. *Be unto me, O Lord, a tower* is in two sections, the first part being a prayer, and the second, which is quicker in tempo, expresses the confidence and joy of the soul relying on God. ' Cheerful ' is as usual pictured in runs, and in this case two parts run together in thirds with an effect almost like that of a nineteenth century anthem. The accentuation of the opening words is noteworthy : Be unto me O Lord a tower— rest and silence in all parts—of strength against my mortal foe ; the harmony meantime moves in solid blocks. There is not very much ' lamentacion of a sorrowful soule ' about this anthem.

The Latin Church music shows one side of Byrd's character, the English church music another. The one shows the stability of the man and his deep-rooted feelings and convictions, the other his enterprise and good sense. The one is assured and masterly, the other is the true pioneer work of an innovator. With the small exceptions already noted in our historical survey of the music immediately preceding Byrd, the English language was not used for musical setting. The Church services were of course sung entirely in Latin, while the madrigals from Italy were in Italian. Byrd's first set of madrigals was not published till 1588 and he had come to London to the Chapel Royal in 1572. The dates of his church compositions are unknown, but some of them must plainly have been written between these two dates. He is therefore the true forerunner of Purcell, Sullivan, Stanford, and Parry in setting the English language. He first discovered its natural rhythm and the melodic shapes required to fit what was more vigorous, less fluent and less sonorous than Latin or Italian.

His use of the organ, in itself something new, also led him into harmonic innovations. Unaccompanied voices even after centuries of acclimatisation, find it difficult to sing swift modulations in tune, and in Byrd's day it was unthinkable that anything like what we call chromatic[1] harmony should be written for them. But there was a very strong tendency to make all the church modes[2] approximate towards the Ionian and Aeolian, our major and minor (melodic form), due to the influence of folk-song, the troubadours, and the dictates of the human ear which made themselves felt in the rules of Musica Ficta.[3] The result was that composers at that

---

[1] Chromatic—literally 'coloured'; it means proceeding by the use of semitones.

[2] The modes are scales which vary in character according to the arrangement of their tones and semitones—the same difference as between major and minor, only there were more of them.

[3] 'Fudged' music. Certain intervals like the tritone (three whole tones) have always been repulsive to the ear and in the modes in which they occur, e.g., the F. or Lydian, singers modified them by sharpening or flattening one note of the interval. This fudging was known as *Musica Ficta.*

time were striving to get away from the modes into diatonic harmony in much the same way as composers are nowadays trying to reverse the process and escape from harmony back into modality. But when they got into major and minor modes the modern feeling for key made itself felt, and composers began to modulate tentatively in the modern style. This, however, could not be done safely by voices unaccompanied, as forbidden or difficult intervals would be involved. As soon, however, as the organ could be used independently this new world could be safely explored. And as we have seen in the case of the anthem, *O Lord, rebuke me not*, Byrd launched out into this uncharted region.

CHAPTER V

BYRD is the first great composer to write music for keyboard instruments. He had his predecessors—all pioneers have—but they have left very little trace of their work behind. Hugh Aston's Hornepype we have already heard of (p. 28), and Tallis's two sets of variations on a plain-song. About 120 pieces for the virginals by Byrd survive to-day. They consist of dances such as pavans and galliards, of which there are over forty, corantos and almans, of variations on songs of the day, of which there are some fifteen, of fantasias (i.e., fugal compositions) on plain-song tunes, of which there are also fifteen, of preludes and miscellaneous pieces. All of these show instrumental style developed to a greater or less degree away from the vocal music which was its parent, and enough variety of treatment to prove that the new art though young was not exactly new-born. But if there were writers of secular instrumental music between Aston and Byrd, as seems possible from this variety and high degree of development which we find in Byrd, their work can hardly have been of much intrinsic value or it would certainly have survived. For, more than 620 compositions by Byrd and his immediate juniors have survived in manuscripts which date back to 1590. Scribes who took the trouble to write out the music they wanted would assuredly have included some of earlier writers if they had liked their work sufficiently. An alternative supposition is that there was really very little music for virginals written down before Byrd's time, and that however much extemporisation there may have been, Byrd is absolutely the first composer to treat this branch of music seriously. In this case he has a greater claim than ever to the title of pioneer. In any case there is nothing like the long ancestry behind the instrumental music as there is behind the choral music of the period, and as a result there is a greater proportion of experimental work which does not satisfy modern ears than in the choral music where the touch is always sure.

There is one other possibility. Just as madrigals came from Italy to kindle the English genius for choral music, so, it may be, from Spain came the first models of instrumental composition to give shape to the English skill in playing the instruments of the Tudor period. Lutes, viols, and organs were played vigorously enough in Henry VIII's day, and the little virginals were in domestic use. In Spain there was a great player of the organ and the clavichord, Cabezon, who was born in 1510 and flourished through the

middle of the sixteenth century. There is a
story that he visited England in the train of
Philip II, who came to marry Queen Mary. If
he did he would certainly have shown his skill
and the music that he wrote to Tallis and the
other Court musicians of the time, who would
have copied it and taught it to their pupils.
But even supposing he did not come at all, there
was a good deal of intercourse between England
and Spain all through the latter part of the
century. Jesuit priests came over to succour
English Catholics and to work against the growing Protestantism of all ranks of English society.
This clandestine intercourse with foreigners
and Englishmen in exile appears on the surface
of Byrd's own life at least twice. There was the
secret celebration of Roman rites at the house of
Mr. Bold related by Father Weston (see p. 81 and
p. 197), and there was William Shelley's original
imprisonment which followed upon the visit of
the Jesuits, Robert Parsons and Edmund Campion,
to England in 1580. (See p. 203n.) We may be
sure, therefore, that the Catholic community in
England, of which Byrd was a member, was in
close touch with Continental Catholics. And
we may also be sure that neither the Inquisition
nor the Society of Jesus was prepared to lose
England without bestirring itself and seeing
to it that there were plenty of missionaries to
support the faithful in this country. It is no
unlikely supposition that Jesuit priests might

8

bring over service music and at the same time specimens of the secular keyboard music of great Spanish organists and court musicians like Cabezon.

Mr. van den Borren in *The Sources of Keyboard Music in England* assumes it as a certain fact that Cabezon did come to England. But he holds that he received quite as much from English musicians as he gave to them. He was a greater creative artist than Tallis, at any rate in the field of instrumental music (as we may test for ourselves by playing over the variations on the *Gallard Milanesa* and the Variations on *El Canto del Caballero* quoted by Pedrell[1]), but the works which are ascribed to the years subsequent to his visit to England are adorned with richer figuration than his earlier keyboard pieces which are less figured than Tallis's. He seems therefore to have been a debtor rather than a creditor to the English in this respect. On the other hand he certainly wrote variations on secular folk-songs before anyone in England thought of doing so, e.g., the Cavalier's Song referred to above; and in the *Gallard Milanesa* he shows a sense of musical form in advance of anything to be found at the date of his death (1566). This galliard consists of two 8-bar strains A and B, which are developed in the following elaborate form :

[1] *Antología de Organistas Clásicos Españoles*, Vol. I. The complete works of Cabezon printed in modern notation from the original tablature may be found in Vols. 3-8 of Pedrell's *Hispaniae Schola Musica Sacra* (Barcelona, 1894).

A (8 bars), B (8+2 bars), A1 (8 bars), A2 (8 bars), B1 (8+2 bars), B2 (8+2 bars), cadence coda (1 bar).

[N.B. The extra bars of the strain B are accounted for by the very odd progression of keys and the last little coda is required by the same necessity of bringing the piece to an end on the right chord.]

The usual form for a dance variation among English writers is A, A1, B, B1, C, C1. The recurrence to A after the enunciation of B is an advance on anything contemporary in England, and may well have been the starting point for Byrd's experiments in form, among which are to be found examples of reversions· to a phrase already treated. These two elements—the annexation of folk-song as a subject for instrumental variation and some hint of form—Byrd may therefore owe indirectly to Cabezon, but it does very little to discount the magnitude of his achievement in evolving by his own single genius an independent instrumental style. This achievement is so great—greater probably than any other single innovation in the history of music except the original discovery of vocal counterpoint in the tenth century—that it has been denied on the ground of the mere improbability of one man being able to accomplish so much. But it is not impossible for one who, like Byrd or Monteverde, combined a careful conservatism of existing resources with boldness in experimenting—qualities which he showed in every branch of his work. He was the genius needed by his time to weld all the elements together and out of them to make a new art form.

Of these elements some half dozen may be distinguished. The old vocal counterpoint which produced Tallis's *Felix Namque* in the Fitzwilliam book provides the fundamental technique of composition ; the bridge between this kind of counterpoint and the virginal music which we know, was the organ—No. 26 of the Nevell book with its fugal suggestion and merry pastoral feeling might very well owe its origin to this influence. Akin to this was the music for consorts of viols, still contrapuntal but beginning to evolve a character of its own more nimble than vocal music. Lute playing was a tendency operating in the direction of harmony and would account for the progression of chords which we often find in the opening sections of pavans and similar dance forms. Beside the aristocratic dancing of the Court there is an unmistakable folk-dance element, not only in things like Sellinger's Round but e.g., in No. 29 of the Nevell Book where, sandwiched between two sections in quite different styles, is a typical English country dance. This dance element brought regular rhythm into music, a revolution quite as great as the change from the modes into tonal harmony. Lastly the nature of the instrument itself helped to mould the music composed for it—organists having under their fingers the lighter keys of the virginal keyboard were not slow to explore the possibilities of rapid figuration into which, encouraged by the example of Italian writers like A. Gabrieli and Merulo, they plunged so wholeheartedly as to leave us of a later time, sated with the festoons of Chopin and the fireworks of Liszt, a little supercilious at their delight in scales. All these styles we find embedded in Byrd's virginal music, and in the best of it fused into a real and new instrumental style.

Some of Byrd's virginal music as well as that of his younger contemporaries, Bull and Gibbons, is even to this day still in manuscript. A very small amount by these three composers was published during their lifetime in a small collection of twenty-one pieces entitled *Parthenia or The Maydenhead of the first musicke that ever was printed for the virginalls*, which came out in 1611. But far more representative both of the period and of the work of individual composers is the *Fitzwilliam Virginal Book*, a manuscript containing 297 compositions by over thirty different composers excluding the prolific Anon., which was copied some time between 1600 and 1620 but did not get into print until 1899. This work, the writing of which beguiled the imprisonment of its editor and copyist, provides enough material for a critical history of the keyboard music from about 1560 to 1620, but it is not the only manuscript collection of pieces. There are besides : Lady Nevell's Book, containing forty-two pieces all by Byrd ;[1] Benjamin Cosyn's Book, with ninety-eight pieces by three composers including Byrd ; and Will Forster's Virginal Book, containing seventy-eight pieces. There are in addition a number of manuscripts in the British Museum, Christ Church Library and the Bodleian Library at Oxford, Paris Conservatoire, and New York Public Library, which contain virginal music.

Lady Nevell's is the earliest in date. At the end of the book the copyist has added the triumphant inscription ' finished and ended the leventh of September in the yeare of our Lorde God 1591 and in the 33 yeare of the raigne of our sofferaine ladie Elizabeth by the grace of God queene of Englande etc, by me Jo. Baldwine of Windsore. Laus Deo.' It therefore represents work which Byrd had written in the earlier part of his career before the mysterious break in his activity, and contains the pavan and galliard which are described in the margin of the Fitz-william Book where they also occur as, 'the first that ever hee made '. They are not bad for a beginner, though the galliard is more pleasing to listen to than the pavan ; they show an advance in the handling of the material upon Blitheman's and Parson's pieces, which are the only things in the

---

[1] Published for the first time in 1926 by Curwen ; edited by Miss H. Andrews.

Fitzwilliam book which may be older. This musical ability even when the results are aesthetically barren is characteristic of Byrd, who is less tempted than many of the virginalists of the time to run wildly up and down the keyboard in sheer delight at the newly found joys of speed in music.

Of the seven pieces in Lady Nevell's Book which are not found elsewhere *The Battle* is an early piece of programme music depicting army life. It is in three sections, of which the first is *The Earle of Oxford's Marche*, found also in the *Fitzwilliam Book* and recorded for gramophone by Mrs Gordon Woodhouse (H.M.V. E294). This " marche before the battel ", as it is called in Lady Nevell's Book, begins dully enough with reiterations of one or two chords in root position, but a picture is gradually set up thereby of men marching and counter-marching, and in the variations which follow fanfares of trumpets and the beating of drums are suggested, all within the limited resources of legitimate virginal technique. It has to be borne in mind that the instrument for which this music was written was not the modern piano with its rather thick tone, which makes reiterated chords sound dead and exasperating. Played on a harpsichord they emit a sparkle, and the plucking of the string by the quill makes a lively sound quite unlike the impact of a hammer ; in the tenor register the tone of a harpsichord, though evanescent, has a quality something like an organ diapason and in the higher registers the brightness of little bells. So that all this battle music is not so crude as it seems when played over on the piano. Repeated figures have the brilliance of fanfares, and reiterated chords have a greater impetus than the thicker tone of the piano can produce, even allowing for the absence of accent. To remedy the lack of sustaining power and the inability to mark a strong accent the virginalists invented numerous ornaments by which to call attention to individual notes. If these are all played out in full on a modern piano the outline is covered up, and it is advisable to discard most of them.

The second section of the Battle Piece consists of the following episodes :

The souldiers sommons, in which the hurly-burly on the parade ground is indicated by plodding steps and hurrying skirmishes in both hands, with the trumpet-call sounding over and over again in the tenor register.

The marche of footemen is a military march with side-drum accompaniment suggested.

The marche of horsmen is in triple time for contrast and depicts the cantering of cavalry. It is a jolly little piece of music ; at the end of it is written " now folowethe the trupetts ".

The trumpetts is a long variation on the chord of C in which the trumpet figure of the " summons " is heard, and in which by a reiteration of single notes the " lipping " of brass instruments is realistically portrayed.

The Irishe marche follows and, it has been suggested, may represent the approach of the enemy, for the Munster risings were recent history (1578-83). The tune is very like " Lillibulero " which Purcell called " The New Irish Tune " in a volume of harpsichord music published a hundred years later.

The bagpipe and the drone is a delightful little movement, not flamboyant but with a gay swinging rhythm.

The flute and the droome shows that Byrd anticipated effects which Tschaikowsky and Holst, composers who have followed him in writing music descriptive of war, have also used to produce feelings of excitement ; a persistent drum rhythm is set up and relentlessly maintained ; the fifers gradually climb higher, but underneath the drum taps go straight on until the last bar.

The marche to the fighte is one long crescendo of movement. It sticks doggedly to the chord of C major for more than two-thirds of its length and there are plenty of trumpet-calls answering one another, until after the soldiers have begun to break into a run there is an excited outburst of repeated notes with " tantara tantara " written into the score. The commotion of the fight begins and under the serried handfuls of quaver chords is written " the battles be joyned " ; the perturbed movement continues till the army advances with a run of semi-quavers and stops.

The retreat follows, in which the movement gets

quicker as it gets farther away ; it must be played with a diminuendo on the piano, though on the virginals that would not have been possible, and Byrd must have relied for his effect of decreasing excitement on four bars of descending scale passages in the bass.

At this point it is convenient to insert (as the editor of the recent edition has done) three pieces which seem to belong to this battle suite though they are not found in the Nevell manuscript nor in the incomplete Christ Church copy, but occur elsewhere ;[1]

The buriing of the dead, in which there is a suggestion of a muffled peal of bells.

The morris—a simple, not very distinguished, but cheerful strain.

Ye souldiers dance, in which the capering of the soldiers is depicted in a jaunty six-in-a-bar measure.

The final ' galliarde for the victorie ' is a separate section like the opening march, and like it will stand as music.

The descriptive middle sections bear witness to a tendency against which no composer seems proof. It is a universal admission that music cannot describe events ; it can portray states of mind, and it can imitate the sounds of Nature or of the world of men only within the limitation that the more it resembles the sound the less it resembles music. Composers know the limitations

[1] Paris MS., 18546.

of their art, but even the greatest ignore them at some point or other in their career—Bach with his *Departure of a beloved brother* and Beethoven with his *Battle of Vittoria*.

The pieces in the Nevell book are worth examination because they show how far Byrd had developed in this new field by 1591. We may glance first at the other numbers which are peculiar to this volume. *The Barelye Breake* (No. 6) is one of the jolliest pieces Byrd ever wrote. It is a medley of thirteen sections, all gay in feeling, containing some in folk-dance rhythm, one with striking harmony in which different tonalities are set side by side without modulation quite in the modern manner but unlike the classical harmony which had then not yet arrived and has now departed. The music reflects the open-air jollity of the barley-break which was a country game and dance. It shows unity of feeling but not of structure. *A Galliards Gygge* is sprightly as befits its title, with plenty of keyboard figuration running through the plucked chords which mark the dance. No. 26 is a *Voluntarie* written specially " for my ladye nevell ". As its name implies its style is derived from the organ, being contrapuntal and full of imitations, though it has not the severity of organ music. *The Second Grownd* (No. 30) has a good " grownd " (i.e., bass part) but is dull music, interesting chiefly from the point of view of virginal technique—one variation for example being a study in thirds and sixths. The last piece in the book (No. 42) is another *Voluntairie* smoothly flowing in organ style and having the grave sweetness characteristic of its composer.

Coming now to the numerous pieces which are common to this and to the Fitzwilliam collections, No. 8 is called *The Huntes Up* in both books, though it appears a second time in the Fitzwilliam book under the title *Pescodd Time*. It is a set of variations on a ground bass, a form of composition much used a hundred years later by Purcell, consisting of repetitions of the same bass part with different tunes and harmony above it. This is not a happy example; the bass is sticky and the composition as a result dull. The 'Passamezzo' pavan and galliard are more interesting, at any rate to play, and contain plenty of harmonic and rhythmic variety. They are disconcerting to hear, owing to the brusque way in which major and minor contradict one another and flats and sharps swear at each other. In these early pieces Byrd is still a long way from the classical harmony based on key, and a little way from the rhythm of recurring accents. Barring had no rhythmic significance at this period and bore no relation to the time signature (which referred only to the proportionate values of the notes to each other, whether e.g. two or three minims were to make up a semibreve). It was merely a convenience to the eye, and the bars in the same composition often varied in length according to the amount of movement (such as ornaments and quaver passages) that was going on. The virginals and the organ, it must be remembered, were incapable of a dynamic accent, and the result is that the music written for them has not the steady march of Bach and all later music. One of the excitements of playing the music of the virginal books, unless they are specially edited, is to feel the changes of grouping as the music goes along. Rhythm in vocal music was determined by the words, in instrumental by the grouping of notes. In modern music the grouping is made round a strong accent, but where there is no such accent to organize the groups, the ear is dependent on periodicity alone on which to build its rhythm. Hence in playing Byrd it is as a rule necessary to make the duration of the single beat the rhythmic basis, and to make one's phrasing depend on the melodic curve. The Passamezzo Pavan provides an example of the unit (a minim) remaining constant while its internal economy is changed from two to three crotchets. Such a change would be described in modern terms as a change from simple to compound time, and the aesthetic effect is a quickening of pace (whether the actual speed is increased or no). This explains a Shakespearian allusion to music. In *Twelfth Night* (V, i, 197) the Clown says that the doctor is drunk early in the day, ' his eyes were set at eight i' the morning '. The word ' set ' sends Sir Toby off on a musical tack: ' Then he's a rogue, and a *passy-measures pavin*'. The passa-mezzo (passy-measures or passinge mesures) was the Italian equivalent of the pavan, but it went a little quicker so that the sweeping steps had to be cut short and it got more lively apparently as it went on. Hence Sir Toby means that the doctor was very quick in his intoxication, and the passa-mezzo pavan means a pavan that got livelier towards the end.[1]

The pavan and the galliard were the two most important dances of the period and most favoured by the virginalists. The pavan is a stately dance—the word is derived from *pavone* =peacock—in quadruple measure ; the galliard which frequently followed it was a quicker but still graceful dance in triple time. Both gave great scope for using the big costumes of the period—the hooped skirts of the women and the cloaks of the men—to good purpose, while the ornamental cadences could be interpreted by little flourishes of the hands and so on.[2] The conjunction of these two dances, which strictly ought to consist of the same musical material in different rhythms but which in practice as often did not, is a foreshadowing of the instrumental suite of later times, and the resemblance is

[1] See Naylor, *An Elizabethan Virginal Book*, p. 33.

[2] I saw in the autumn of 1925 at a concert given by the Misses Chaplin a pavan and galliard danced by two couples, who showed exactly how this music came to be written. Whether their dancing was correct or not choreographically I have no idea, but it fitted the music and *interpreted* it perfectly.

increased when, as happens in *Parthenia*, a Prelude is pre-fixed.

Next for consideration and common to the Nevell and the Fitzwilliam books are the variations on *The Woods so Wild*, a catchy popular song of the period. This tune was also set by Orlando Gibbons (*Fitz.*, No. XL); Byrd's version[1] is actually dated 1590. There are thirteen variations on the tune, which is only four bars (of 12-8 time) long. How does Byrd do it ? The contrapuntal ingenuities of Tallis, Blitheman and Parsons represent the kind of thing which had been woven round fragments of plain song for long enough, but there is no example earlier than this of variations in the modern sense, and variations moreover of a secular tune, except in the examples from Spain mentioned above. What Byrd does may be set out briefly in a table as follows :

1. Tune stated.
2. Tune an octave higher : slight changes in harmony.
3. Tune put into the alto.
4. Tune absent ; a figure derived from the second bar of the tune is tossed about in imitation.
5. Tune still absent : this variation is similar to No. 4 but a little more elaborate.
6. Tune reappears in the treble, with decorative runs in the treble.
7. Tune in treble ; three-part harmony instead of four ; decorative bass.

---

[1] It may be found in Bantock's collection of twelve pieces published by Novello.

8. Original bass present, tune absent; figures in imitation.
9. Only general outlines of tune and harmony recognisable; imitative figures between treble and bass.
10. Original bass : decorations in form of runs suited to keyed instruments.
11. A mixture of several previous variations : the original bass is kept, the rhythmic figure of bar two is tossed about in imitation alternately with passages of runs.
12. The bass mostly the same, the tune partly quoted in the tenor, a slight change of harmony at the end.
13. Tune in the alto, old harmony.
14. Re-statement of tune in treble, varied and fuller harmony; a brief coda added.

Several points in this scheme are worthy of note because they foreshadow later developments. First there is the general sense of form of the whole, obtained by stating the tune clearly at the beginning and end but departing from it in the middle. This is the germ from which sonata form developed, and the coda looks forward to Beethoven. Variations 4 and 5 are perhaps the most interesting of all, because they contain the hint of what in later times came to be called 'development'. The principle of the ground bass is involved in nos. 8, 10, 11 and 12. No. 11 is an example of material being combined as in the 'working-out' section of a sonata. Lastly there is a feeling towards harmonic

variation.   The tune itself is not really in F major
but in the Lydian mode.[1]   Being a popular song
its accompaniment (if any) would be played on the
lute or other stringed instrument descended from
those used by the troubadours.   The lute from
its nature tends to provide support for the voice
in the form not of counterpoint but of chords.
This was one of the forces making in the direction
of modern harmony, and in *The Woods so Wild*
one can feel the way in which an enterprising bass
part pushed a modal tune in that direction.

The other contents of *My Lady Nevell's
Booke* must be dealt with more rapidly.   *The
Maydens Song* is a set of contrapuntal variations
on a rather jolly tune which begins oddly enough
in the tenor, as though the mayden had a very
deep contralto voice, and goes through every
register of the keyboard.   It contains a variation
in which there is an extraordinary combination
of duple and triple rhythms such as would have
appealed to Brahms if he knew the piece.

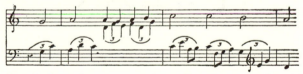

Byrd has been not inaptly compared with
Schumann in this piece with its vigorous yet

[1] N.B. the B natural in the second bar ; but note also how in accordance
with Musica Ficta the B flat is twice substituted when the B falls to an A ;
the chord of D major in the last bar is a permitted modulation in the Lydian
mode.

9

romantic tune and imitational treatment. *Walsingham* is a very similar composition founded on a popular melody of pre-Reformation times, also treated by Bull, of a ballad which began :

> As I went to Walsingham
> To the shrine with speed,
> Met I with a jolly palmer
> In a pilgrim's weed.[1]

—Walsingham being a celebrated place of pilgrimage in Norfolk. In Lady Nevell's Book it is called *Have with you to Walsingame*. *All in a garden green, Rowland, The Carman's Whistle* and *Sellinger's Round* are all sets of variations on popular tunes. *Lord Willoughby's Welcome Home* is called *Rowland* in the Fitzwilliam book ; it is recorded for gramophone (H.M.V. E295) and is included in Bantock's selection. This is Byrd in his most charming vein. There is a little repeated figure which gives the piece a touch of playfulness. The tune is in two sections, and like a modern symphonist Byrd begins to ' develop ', i.e. to vary, it before he has enunciated the whole of it, so that the form of the theme is A (2 bars), A', B (4 bars)[2] B', and on this complete theme there are two variations both quite simple. The composer has completely unbent and entertains his hearers with a grace that is almost feminine for him.

---

[1] Cf. *Oxford Book of English Verse*, No. 26 : " ' As ye came from the holy land of Walsinghame ', which is not a ballad but for the first eight verses looks like a folk-song in semi-dramatic form, the last three verses, however, being more sophisticated.

[2] Two bars in the original notation, four in most modern editions.

The Lord Willoughby whose name is borrowed, was an English captain who had defeated the Spaniards in Flanders. As we have already seen it was a favourite practice of the time to name these small pieces after notable people, just as it was the custom to dedicate the larger published works to powerful patrons. *The Carman's Whistle*,[1] one of the most famous of all virginal pieces, is another little work of a light and immediately captivating character. Carmen in general had the reputation for whistling original tunes, and this carman in particular is said to have consoled a pretty maiden in distress with this cheerful tune and its pert syncopations. Byrd in his quiet way was quite capable of entering into the fun of a tune of this sort, and could make contrapuntal variations on it without marring its simplicity. Perhaps as a joke he adds at the end a different kind of variation where there is only a suggestion of the tune and which ought to be marked *grandioso*. This pompous section follows a graceful variation in two parts and makes a climax for the work to end on. *Sellinger's*[2] *Round* is another popular piece of a jolly character. This is a dance measure, 'round' meaning not the form of vocal composition also so called, but a round dance like the French 'ronde'. The variations are, however, more elaborate and

---

[1] Also included in Bantock's edition.

[2] Sellinger—Saint Leger, either the place in Cornwall or the family of that name.

131

include one or two which we should nowadays describe as pianistic—one being a study in thirds. Another round also by Byrd only to be found in the Fitzwilliam book, is the *Gipseis Round*. This is a simple and pleasant piece, but more monotonous harmonically owing to long-held notes in the bass, tonic and subdominant mainly, which serve however to give a pastoral flavour to the piece as though they were the drones of a pipe. A set of variations on a ground common to the Nevell and the Fitzwilliam books, though of no special musical or æsthetic value, has a double personal interest, in that it is called ' Hughe Aston's grounde ' in the Neville book and ' Treg. ground ' in the Fitzwilliam. Treg. is short for Tregian, and Tregian is the name of the man who in all probability made the Fitzwilliam collection. His story is worth telling, as it throws a sidelight on the life of the times. The Fitzwilliam Book is supposed to be in the handwriting of Francis Tregian, who was imprisoned in the Fleet prison from 1608 till his death in 1619. The reason of his imprisonment was his Roman Catholicism, which had also been the undoing of his father before him. The Tregians were a wealthy Cornish family. In the seventies of the sixteenth century more than at the present time unpopular opinions marked men out as fair game. There was therefore a plot to ruin a family which was both rich and Roman Catholic. Their house was searched and a young priest who acted as steward to the elder Francis Tregian was arrested, convicted of high treason and executed with hideous barbarity. 'Tregian himself who had been bound over to appear at the Assizes was committed a close prisoner to the Marshalsea, where he remained for ten months. He was then suddenly arraigned before the King's Bench and sent into Cornwall to be tried. For some time the jury would deliver no verdict, but after having been repeatedly threatened by the judges, a conviction was obtained, and Tregian was sentenced to suffer the penalty of præmunire and perpetual banishment. . . Immediately judgement was given he was laden with irons and thrown into the common county gaol; his goods were seized, his wife and children expelled from their home and his mother was deprived of her jointure. After being moved from prison to prison and suffering indignities without number, Tregian was finally confined in the Fleet, where his wife joined him. He remained in prison for twenty-four years.'[1] In 1606 he was able to leave England and he died two years later in Lisbon. Francis Tregian the younger was educated abroad but was rash enough to return to England and to buy back some of his father's estate. He was accused of recusancy[2] and suffered ten years' imprisonment for it, and it was to while away his time in prison

---

[1] Quoted from the introduction to the 1899 edition of the *Fitz-william Book* by J. A. Fuller-Maitland and W. Barclay Squire.

[2] A recusant was one who refused to conform to the English church.

133

that he wrote out this huge collection of music. To this monstrous iniquity then we owe this priceless manuscript. It is a consolation to reflect that Byrd himself, though frequently summoned as a recusant, never seems to have suffered anything very serious for his faith, through all the increasing Protestantism of his long life. In English histories the persecutions of the Protestant reaction are usually glossed over, so that it comes as something of a shock to encounter so bad a case at first hand, which does go to show that the famous remark of the Catholic encyclopædist is not the mere fantastic nonsense that it appears to be on the ordinary reading of the events of the time : ' the religious persecutions of Henry the Eighth's and Edward the Sixth's time abated a little in the reign of Mary, to break out again with new fury in the reign of Elizabeth.'

Of the seventy-two compositions by Byrd in the Fitzwilliam book there remain a few requiring special commentary, though the best of the sets of variations have already been mentioned. *O Mistris Myne* begins and ends with the straightforward enunciation of the tune which is associated with the love song in *Twelfth Night*. The intermediate sections consist of florid writing and considerable rhythmic complications that appealed to the virtuoso performer in Byrd, who however never went to the lengths of virtuosity of his younger contemporary Bull, who seems to have been a sixteenth-century Liszt. The earliest

A PAGE OF THE FITZWILLIAM MANUSCRIPT SHOWING
THE BELLS

(Fitzwilliam Museum)

[*face p. 135*

record of the tune is 1599, the year in which Shakespeare wrote *Twelfth Night,* and it is by no means impossible that either Byrd or Morley, his pupil who printed it in *The Firste Booke of Consort Lessons made by diverse exquisite authors for six Instruments,* may have collaborated with Shakespeare in the production of the play. *The Bells* also is a set of variations, but of a unique kind. The ' ground ' on which it is founded is simply

which suggests the persistent ringing of the big bell of a peal. Over this, bells great and small, including little silvery chimes (variation 5, e.g.), have the changes rung on them through nine different sections and varying moods. Bells seem to have made a very strong appeal to Byrd; we have seen how in his vocal music he seems to think in terms of bells when he wishes to express joy, and the fact that they had this special significance for him makes this piece not a mere piece of crude imitation but a truly descriptive piece of programme music of the best sort. There is enough realism in the ding-dong of the bass, in the ' ringing up ' and the ' ringing down ' at the beginning and end, in the little figures suggestive of a carillon, and in the descending scales of the ordinary peal to make his impressionistic picture true to life, but there is also much more than this—the reflection of varying moods : sober contentment (§3), impetuosity (§4), tenderness (§6), gaiety (§7), and excitement (§8). Unlike modern users of bell effects Byrd employs no dissonance— in this respect he is not realistic and does not try to reproduce directly the hum of the belfry, and he remains in C major throughout— which makes the piece tiresome to practice. It is a romantic and joyous piece of music, that has great artistic worth because it is all the time keyboard music. None the less it sounds magnificent when transferred to orchestra with bell effects.[1]

Something has already been said of the pavan and galliard which are the most important of the dance measures which Byrd requisitioned for keyboard use. *Parthenia* contains two pavans : one with the title *S. Wm Petre* intersperses each strain with scale passages that sound rather futile and tiresome to our more sophisticated ears; the other, *The Earle of Salisbury*,[2] is a gem. It consists of two simple strains, each repeated ; there are no swift capers for the fingers to cut, only a little marching sequence of five notes, in which one can almost see the dancers executing their steps, earnest and intent on perfection ; yet it is all quite simple-minded and—in one word —exquisite. There is another pavan with the same title by Orlando Gibbons in *Parthenia* on

[1] It has been scored both for orchestra and for military band by Mr. Gordon Jacob. The gramophone record of the latter arrangement gives no idea of the merits of the piece as it is taken far too slowly and is not well recorded. (H.M.V. C1215.)

[2] Printed in Bantock's collection.

rather a bigger scale, also a fine work with a splendid sequential climax, characteristic of its composer and interesting to play alongside of Byrd's. There is a *Pavana Fantasia* by Byrd in the *Fitzwilliam Book* which as its name suggests is fugal in character (the fantasia in Elizabethan times was a contrapuntal composition) ; the points of imitation give it a confortable flowing feeling which is interrupted by sections of wandering scale passages. Byrd also made a ' setting ' of Dowland's famous tune *Lachrymae* (Tears), as did Morley and Farnaby ; all three *Lachrymae* pavans are in the *Fitzwilliam Book*.

Of noteworthy galliards there is a short and simple one immediately following *The Earle of Salisbury* in *Parthenia* which may well belong to it. *Sir John Grayes Galliard*[1] is an attractive little piece, compact and well composed, almost as graceful as Farnaby's writing and breathing the spirit of the open air. A harmonic progression in the middle of it betrays its date even to the unlearned. Its feeling is more strongly of D minor than of the Dorian mode, yet we find a bar in which the harmony throughout is D major in root position followed immediately by the common chord of C major, which of course flings us back with some violence into the old modal way of thinking. This same juxtaposition of chords is responsible for the very curious sound of the opening of a Galliard played on the harpsichord

[1] In Bantock's collection.

by Mrs. Gordon Woodhouse and recorded for gramophone (H.M.V. E295). Mrs. Woodhouse's harpsichord contains what the virginals did not, octave and sub-octave couplers, and with these in action the acidity of the progression is enhanced. The bold masculine character of the first section (which is played twice on the record) is also emphasised by the full tone obtained from the use of the couplers. The middle section is more feminine, but the sturdy runs of the third part restore the original robustness. The piece is No. CCLV in the *Fitzwilliam Book*.

' Alman ', ' coranto ', and 'jigg,' less numerous than pavans and galliards, but next in order of importance, are the same names as appear in Bach as ' allemande ' or German dance, ' courante ' or French running dance, and ' gigue '. The later dances have the same rhythmic foundation as the earlier ones though the character has somewhat changed. The coranto for example is still a triple measure, but whereas Byrd's examples have a strongly marked trochaic rhythm

$$(-\; \flat \; \flat \; | \; \flat \; \flat \;)$$

which gives them a popular feeling in spite of their aristocratic origin, Bach's are of a smoother, more running character in accordance with the name—

$$(-\; \flat \; \flat \; \flat \; | \; \flat \; \flat \;)$$

for instance. The two by Byrd in the Fitzwilliam book are both short and charming in feeling,

138

light-hearted but not exuberant, tripping and
graceful, and extremely simple in construction.
The Alman, like the pavan, is a dance in quadruple
time and similar in its movements only rather
quicker, in fact alman and coranto are like the
pavan and galliard, employing similar steps,
related to each other as quadruple to triple
measure, but are faster. Shakespeare speaks of
swift corantos (*Henry V*, III, v, 32) :

> *Bourbon :* They bid us to the English dancing schools,
> And teach lavoltas high and swift corantos.

Lavolta means the leap and is therefore termed
' high '. Two steps only were danced to the bar
and a leap occurred in every alternate bar. In
the two examples by Byrd there is a little cadence
on which this jump could be made. The music
is thus very much cut up into short sections, but
it moves fast and spryly, so that the effect is not
tiresome but one of simple gaiety, such as the now
forgotten polka used to have before it began to
make its fatal approximation to the valse. The
utter simplicity of the music is captivating, and is
worth remembering to put against the complications and the splendour of his great ecclesiastical
works. There are five almans by Byrd, all with
florid figures for the keyboard woven into the
simple dance strains. The most florid is *The
Queens Alman*, which sounds most brilliant as
played on the harpsichord by Mrs. Gordon
Woodhouse (H.M.V. E294). The piece is indeed

well named, for the crispness of the runs combined
with a certain formal elegance derived from the
dance framework makes a wonderful portrait of
the great Queen. We hear her bandying clever
repartees with her courtiers yet always remaining
the great lady ; we see the dignity and splendour
of the court yet are not oppressed with any stiff-
ness. *Monsieurs Alman* is pleasing in a simpler
manner and is closer to the ordinary type of less
highly developed dance pieces. There is one jig
by Byrd, a short piece in two sections of a sprightly
character, in triplet rhythm and with the feeling
of the country dance exhaled from it. There is
nothing elaborate about it and it only contains
one ornament.[1] The same spirit breathes through
the two lavoltas of Byrd which are found in the
Fitzwilliam book—the feeling of open-air jollity
coupled with the grace of folk-dancing. They are
easy to play, and their simple charm makes them
most suitable for domestic music-making.

Eight pieces by Byrd were included in *Parthenia*,
the first printed music for keyboard, but they were
all in the smaller forms : two pavans, four galliards
and two preludes. The latter were exactly what
their name implies and not the more or less
elaborate compositions which now pass under it:
they were preliminary skirmishes for the fingers.
One is reprinted by Bantock and consists of runs
and little figures in various rhythms founded on a
basis of four notes of the scale. The other

[1] It is included by Bantock in his selection of twelve pieces.

composers represented by similar pieces were Bull (1562-1628) and Gibbons (1583-1625). Of larger pieces there are in the various collections besides the variations already considered, some contrapuntal works of which the interest is mainly theoretical, though in all that Byrd wrote there is discernible that gracious sobriety and the peculiar bitter-sweet tang of his harmony that is so pleasing. Some of this music may very possibly have been designed for the organ. The little *Miserere* in four parts (Bantock, No. VI.), in which the plain-song soon loses itself among the free counterpoint of the parts, contains no figured or rapid passages such as the early virginalists could hardly resist when writing for the little domestic instrument, and would on the other hand sound well on the organ. There are four fantasies by Byrd in the Fitzwilliam Book, all of fair length, in which the composer expends his contrapuntal ingenuity with good effect in the different sections of which these works are made up, but as there is no strong organic connection between the sections, they sound to the modern ear as though they are merely wandering. All Elizabethan fantasies begin like the fugues of a later century, but those of Byrd do not persist very long with a single subject. In one fantasia he makes twelve entries of the subject and the copyist proudly labels them, and he then goes on to other subjects or fragments of subjects which he treats in imitations and echoes and what not. In another he seems to have the madrigal in mind, and though he introduces scale passages and other virginalistic figuring he uses a good deal deal of homophony (i.e. chords in blocks). In these as in the curious pieces entitled *Ut, re, mi fa, sol, la,* and *Ut, mi, re,* the student will find, interesting traces of key feeling. Ut, re, mi, fa, sol, la stand for the first six notes of the modern major scale, and both Byrd and Bull used them as a subject for a piece in which they try experiments in what we should now call modulation, i.e., changes of key. Bull is more reckless than Byrd, who however safely leads the way through a number of both sharp and flat keys.

If we consider all this keyboard music as a whole we are bound to admit that it is not great music even in a small form, as the Church music is great or as the secular madrigals are great. It is not so profound as the one nor so vigorous and assured as the other. Much of it is tentative and hardly interesting to play or to listen to. But much of it, as we have seen, is charming, some of it is gay, a good deal has the grave wistfulness so characteristic of the composer, a little of it is deliciously fanciful and a little is playful. Some of it is brilliant technically and some brilliant in sound. So that within its limited range it expresses considerable variety of mood, and it is interesting to see combined in Byrd qualities which became more marked in his younger contemporaries—the boldness and brilliance of

Bull, the grave severity of Gibbons, and the romantic charm of Farnaby. In this branch of music also he was the founder of a school.

We come now to another class of instrumental music—the works for concerted strings. The great houses of the nobility were well furnished with chests of viols, and ability to play on them seems to have been almost as common as the ability to sing a part. It was a common practice to fill in a voice part of a madrigal on a viol in the absence of a competent singer, and when players wanted something to play they took the madrigals and played them. Byrd, as we shall see, wrote a certain number of madrigals for one or two voices with the other parts specially directed to be played on viols, but he also wrote a certain number of works specially for combinations of viols. Many of these, which have yet to be scored and published, are based on fragments of plain song and are described as In Nomines[1]; there are also several fantasias in various numbers of parts. Byrd published one string fantasia in six parts in his 1611 set of madrigals. Dr. Fellowes has published[2] another one which comes from a MS. in the British Museum, and Sir Richard Terry has edited[3] a five-part fantasia on a secular tune " The leaves be greene " which is mysteriously called " Browning ". These are probably the best of the chamber works, in which department of

[1] See above p. 25 for definition.
[2] Stainer and Bell.   [3] Curwen.

music Byrd has again the honour of being a pioneer.

The string fantasia in six parts (H.M.V. E293) which Byrd published in his 1611 volume of madrigals is constructed like a madrigal, i.e., a single phrase is given out corresponding to the single line of verse which would be fitted with a short piece of tune in a madrigal, it is tossed from one voice to another with accompanying counterpoints, and after its possibilities have been used it comes to a cadence out of which another theme grows to be treated in the same manner. It has not the excursions into passages of finger work of the fantasies for virginals, but it contains a quick middle section which is in true instrumental style. Before this middle section there have been four related themes treated, and after it there is a new theme in triple rhythm but at the original tempo, so that the effect is something like that of the recapitulation of a piece of ternary form. This theme is treated at the greatest length of all, and so the balance of the whole is exactly right : new material, old pace, and in length the two last sections are approximately equal to the first section, while there is a new source of strength to the structure in the shape of a well-defined system of keys. The first part begins in G minor,[1] goes to G major and D major, and then coming back re-establishes flats by a passage in

[1] N.B. When this is performed by modern instruments according to Dr Fellowes's edition of the score the pitch is raised a perfect fourth.

B flat major and so to G minor with a cadence in the tonic major, while the other sections modulate to F major and C major. This cyclic arrangement foreshadows the basis of key on which chamber music came to be built in the time of Haydn. In spite of its being one of the earliest pieces written for concerted viols—it was written before 1611—it is a perfect specimen of its kind. We have already seen how well balanced it is in structure. In feeling it is a perfect pastoral, a light grey haze adding to its sweetness, while the middle section interrupts its placid charm for the moment to add a touch of human interest to the peaceful landscape.

The other six-part fantasia is constructed on similar lines, but is not quite so well wrought. The excursions into different keys are less bravely carried out, though the themes employed are of well-marked character and there are several of them, including 'Greensleeves'. In *The Leaves be greene* the structure is of the older fashion and belongs to the *In nomine* class of composition, though founded on a bright secular tune. The work is scored for strings without voices, but the words 'The leaves be greene, the nutts be browne, They hange soe highe they will not come down' can be fitted to the tune in one part or another throughout the course of the piece, which does however modulate through several keys on a definite cyclic principle : F major (4 statements), C (4), G (2), then back to F, after which it alternates between F and C like the subject and answer of a fugue. It is very smooth sounding counterpoint, begins quietly in a wistful strain, but works up to great richness. There is a four-part fantasia for strings as well as the first six-part fantasia in *Psalms Songs and Sonets* of 1611.

There are one or two compositions of Byrd in lute books in the British Museum, but it is probable that these are arrangements, and it does not seem as though Byrd was drawn to the lute, which was enjoying at the time no less popularity than madrigal singing and instrumental music. John Dowland, one of Byrd's younger contemporaries, wrote some of the finest songs in the English language to the lute ; and when at the end of the sixteenth century the prejudice against broken consorts had finally collapsed, it received a new impetus from the music written by Morley and the seventeenth-century composers like Lawes for lute, viols, recorders and other instruments in different combinations. It did not in fact finally decline in favour till the second half of the seventeenth century, when the violin and harpsichord together made it obsolete. But the fact simply remains that Byrd, not being a singer like Dowland, and being a virtuoso of keyed instruments, left the lute alone.

There was no pioneer work to be done with the lute, and there was no strong compulsion upon him to write songs as there was to write Latin church music in the old manner. Byrd seems to have needed the stimulus either of his own supreme skill in established musical ways or of a healthy curiosity in paving the road that opened in front of him into new country.

CHAPTER VI

In Elizabethan times there were no public concerts. The church music which we have just examined was public music; the rudimentary music for instruments and the early madrigals at which we glanced in Chapter II was private domestic music performed by amateurs. There was nothing corresponding to the modern secular music performed by professionals. The first public concerts in England were given from 1672-1678 by John Banister. Secular music in the time of Byrd therefore was a domestic affair. Yet one of the most striking features of the madrigals which were written to be performed in the home was the difficulty of them. The modern amateur vocalist who can struggle through a drawing-room ballad only by slowing up the rhythm at the awkward places soon finds himself in difficulties if he is handed a madrigal to read at sight, and many competent professional singers find great difficulty in singing the bigger madrigals of Byrd, Weelkes and Gibbons. Yet it seems to have been a fact that after supper it was the usual thing for a hostess to produce a set of part-books —not, be it noted, complete vocal scores such as can now be bought for a few pence, but single parts in which no singer could see, if he lost his place, where the other parts had got to—and to expect her guests to take a part, or if circumstances so required to play it upon a viol. Just as nowadays to be unable to take a hand at bridge is regarded in some circles as a sign of barbarian upbringing, so in the days of Elizabeth and James I it was a social solecism to sit out when the music books were brought to the table. There are several pieces of evidence[1] for the prevalence of what we should now call a high standard of sight singing, of which the most striking is the famous passage from Morley's *Plaine and Easie Introduction to Practicall Musicke*. This, one of the earliest and certainly the most charming text-book of musical theory ever written, was published in 1597, and it begins by describing in dialogue form the discomfiture of an unmusical young man in an oft-quoted passage. Philomathes (which means ' anxious to learn ') is the name of the young man who is hailed by a friend Polymathes (which means ' learned '), and the following conversation occurs.

Polymathes : Staye (brother Philomathes) : What haste? Whither go you so fast ?

Philomathes : To seeke out an old frind of mine.

Polymathes : But before you goe, I praie you repeat some of the discourses which you had yester

[1] There are also several pieces of evidence that the madrigals were often badly performed. Cf. the Introduction to Byrd's own 1611 set, quoted below, p. 182, and the remark of Gibbons quoted in the footnote on p. 155.

night at master *Sophobulus* his banket : For commonly he is not without both wise and learned guestes.

Philomathes : It is true in deede. And yester night, there were a number of excellent schollers (both gentlemen and others :) but all the propose, which then was discoursed upon, was Musicke.

Polymathes : I trust you were contented to suffer others to speake of that matter.

Philomathes : I would that had been the worst : for I was compelled to discouer mine own ignorance, and confesse that I knewe nothing at all in it.

Polymathes : How so ?

Philomathes : Among the rest of the guestes, by chaunce, master *Aphron* came thether also, who falling to discourse of Musicke, was in argument so quickely taken up & hotly pursued by *Eudoxus* and *Calergus*, two kinsmen of *Sophobulus*, as in his owne art he was ouerthrowne. But he still sticking in his opinion, the two gentlemen requested mee to examine his reasons, and confute them. But I refusing, & pretending ignorance, the whole companie condemned mee of discurtesie, being fully perswaded, that I had beene as skilfull in that art, as they tooke mee to be learned in others. But supper being ended, and Musicke bookes according to the custome being brought to the table : the mistresse of the house presented mee with a part, earnestly requesting mee to sing. But when after manie excuses, I protested unfainedly

that I could not: euerie one began to wonder.
Yea, some whispered to others, demaunding
how I was brought up : so that upon shame of
mine ignorance, I go nowe to seeke out mine
olde frinde, master *Gnorimus*, to make my selfe
his scholler.

This is impressive enough until we find that
this kind of thing was a stock method of gilding
the pill of instruction at the period. Another
famous text-book, the *Orchésographie* of Thoinot
Arbeau, a French priest who wrote on dancing
in a similar dialogue form, published nine years
before Morley's treatise, begins on identically the
same lines. The pupil's name is Capriol; this is
how Arbeau begins (only in French) :

Capriol : I come to greet you, M. Arbeau. You do
not remember me, for it is six or seven years
since I departed from this town of Langres to
go to Paris, and from there to Orleans. I am
an old pupil of yours whom you taught
computation.

Arbeau : Certainly at first sight I did not recognize
you, for you have grown vastly since then. I
hope you have likewise broadened your mind
by virtue and knowledge. What do you think
of the study of law ? At one time I myself
studied it.

Capriol : I find that it is a beautiful art, and one very
necessary to the ordering of public affairs, but I
regret that when at Orleans I neglected to learn
the art of good manners which so many scholars

acquire at the same time as their serious studies; because on my return I found myself in a society in which I was forced to remain dumb, unable to speak or move, and regarded as little more than a block of wood.

Arbeau : But you derived consolation in that the learned doctors excused this failing while mindful of the learning you had acquired.

Capriol : That is so, but I should have liked to acquire the art of dancing in the leisure hours between my studies ; it is an accomplishment that would have made my company agreeable to everyone.[1]

We might therefore well hesitate to accept Morley's introduction as evidence of the prevalence of musical culture in society if it was the only reference of the kind, and might easily discount it on the ground that Morley was adopting a common literary fiction of the period and was using the method of suggestion to puff his own wares in the spirit of good modern advertising. But in a book of etiquette called *The Compleat Gentleman* published by Henry Peacham in 1622 music is included among the necessary accomplishments of a gentleman along with falconry, archery and heraldry. These are Peacham's explicit words :

'I desire no more in you than to sing your part sure and at the first sight ; withall, to play

[1] Quoted by kind permission from the translation of C. W. Beaumont, 1925.

152

the same upon your violl, or the exercise of the lute, privately to yourself.' Doubtless the royal enthusiasm for every kind of music helped to establish the practice of singing Italian madrigals in Henry VIII's reign[1] and gave the amazing impetus to the composition of English madrigals in the reign of Elizabeth, for the royal example would be followed in the upper walks of society and in those large country houses to which Elizabeth was wont to pay visits. Madrigal singing could hardly, however, have been a craze until the fifteen-nineties, for Byrd in his first volume (1588) prefaced it with eight 'Reasons briefly set down by th' auctor, to perswade every one to learne to sing.' And in the Epistle to the Reader of the same volume, part of which has already been quoted, he is tender for the inexperienced singer: 'If thou desire songs of small compasse and fit for the reach of most voyces heere are most in number of that sort'. But the fashion spread rapidly, for we find him publishing a second set in the following year in which he refers, both in the dedication and in his address 'to the curteous Reader', to the increase in the practice of the Art. His dedication (to Sir Henry Carye) begins: 'Having observed (Right Honorable) that since the publishing in print, of my last labors in Musicke, divers persons of great honor and worship, have more esteemed and delighted in the exercise of that Art, then

[1] As we have seen (p. 17), the king himself could sing from music at sight.

153

beefore. And beeing perswaded that the same hath the rather encreased, through their good acceptation of my former endevours : it hath especially moved and encouraged mee to take further paines to gratifie theyr curteous dispositions thereunto, knowing that the varietie and choise of songs, is both a praise of the Art, and a pleasure to the delighted therein '. And in similar terms he addresses the courteous reader: 'Finding that my last Impression of Musicke (most gentle Reader) through thy curtesie and favour, hath had good passage and utterance : and that since the publishing thereof, the exercise and love of that Art to have been exceedingly encreased. I have been encouraged thereby, to take further paines therein, and to make thee pertaker thereof, because I would shew my selfe grateful to thee for thy love, and desirous to delight thee with varietie, whereof (in my opinion) no Science is more plentifully adorned then Musicke. For which purpose I do now publish for thee, songs of 3, 4, 5 and 6 parts, to serve for all companies and voices : whereof some are easie and plaine to sing, other more hard and difficult, but all, such as any yong practicioner in singing, with a litle foresight, may easely performe.' A few years later Byrd's juniors, his pupils some of them, began to publish sets, and between 1593 and 1627 over forty collections appeared, testifying in the most practical manner to the great demand that by this time existed for domestic English vocal music.

We of the present day, who find sight-singing so difficult in spite of all the machinery of sight-tests at competition festivals and in schools, and our widespread ability to play the piano, look enviously at the proficiency of our forefathers in singing, saying to ourselves ' How can these things be ? ' That there was a very remarkable proficiency is hardly to be denied—the mere demand and the supply of new music which met the demand are evidence enough of that. But we may easily exaggerate the Elizabethan powers of sight-singing. Byrd, it will be noticed, speaks of ' a little foresight ', which is not quite the same thing as singing at sight, and in the introduction to his 1611 volume he remarks that a song ' is seldome or never well performed at the first singing or playing '—which is only what any musician knows.[1] At the same time, without assigning miraculous powers to them, it is certain that if they sang these madrigals at all frequently they would quickly become familiar with the idiom and would acquire considerable facility in reading them at sight, just as lay-clerks in cathedrals by dint of daily practice can sing church music without much rehearsal. The vogue for madrigal singing at the end of the sixteenth century spread to England from Italy. The Italians, under the impetus of the Renaissance, had developed the

[1] See also the remark of Gibbons : ' Experience tels us that Songs of this Nature are usually esteemed as they are well or ill performed, which excellent grace I am sure your unequalled love unto Musicke will not suffer them to want, that the Author (whom you no lesse love) may be free from disgrace.'

art of writing and singing madrigals fifty years before. They had learned it from the Flemish writers Willaert, Arcadelt and Roland de Lattre, who is always known under his Italian name, Orlando di Lassus. These in their turn owed much to a great Englishman of the previous century, John Dunstable (c. 1400-53), so that though the Englishman of the sixteenth owed much to the Italians it was but the repayment of an earlier debt. But the practice of madrigal singing in England began with the singing of Italian madrigals imported for the purpose. Dr Fellowes describes[1] a set of part-books now at Winchester College containing about seventy part-songs of the Flemish and Italian school with Italian words and a few French chansons, which is dated 1564, and in 1588—the same year as Byrd's first publication—we have the volume of Italian madrigals called *Musica Transalpina* (Music from over the Alps) issued by Nicholas Yonge,[2] at whose house the gentlemen and merchants used to meet for ' the exercise of Musicke daily '. The popularity of Italian madrigals continued even after the great stream of English music was in full flow, for Yonge published another volume in 1595. But if Italian specimens continued to be produced after English composition had become well established, the English had by way of compensation begun to invade the Italian monopoly before the time of Byrd.

[1] *English Madrigal Composers*, p. 38.   [2] See above p. 46.

As early as 1530 Wynkyn de Worde had published a set of part-books (madrigals were never published in score at this period), and there were in the middle of the century a few secular songs by Cornish and even by Tye and Tallis. In the Mulliner MS. there is the famous madrigal *In going to my naked bed* which is often heard now and which is widely known from the inclusion of the words in many anthologies. This is at least as early as 1564. The only other English madrigals of any account before Byrd were a set of seventy-six *Songs of three fower and five voyces*, by Thomas Wythorne published in 1571. The other composers of the middle of the century like Taverner, Tallis and Tye seem to have found themselves fully occupied in serving the church during its repeated upheavals. There are few secular songs of theirs in existence, and they may have composed music for the stage plays in which the boys of the Chapel Royal were often engaged for the amusement of the Court. But though Byrd cannot be regarded as an inventor of a new form of music, he was the father and founder of the great school of madrigal writers which is one of the glories of the Elizabethan epoch. A father himself, he was the child of the English secular song on the one side and the Italian madrigals on the other; but he stamped his work with his own personality and in so far as he made the madrigal a new thing he may be regarded as the pioneer who laid the last, though not the first, bit of road that leads to this particular mansion in the heavenly city of Music.

Byrd's first volume of madrigals bears the following inscription upon its title-page : *Psalmes, Sonets & songs of Sadnes and | pietie, made into Musicke of five parts ; whereof, | some of them going abroad among divers, in untrue coppies | are heere truely corrected, and th' other being Songs | very rare and newly composed, are heere published, for the recreation | of all such as delight in Musicke* : ' By William Byrd | one of the Gent of the Queenes Maiesties | honorable Chappell. | Printed by Thomas East the assigne of W. Byrd, | and are to be sold at the dwelling house of the said T. East, by Paules Wharfe. | 1588 | cum privilegio Regiae Maiestatis.' There then follow the ' Reasons briefely set downe by th' auctor, to perswade euery one to learne to sing ' to which reference has already been made. They must be quoted here, as they give one of the none too many glimpses we have of the man from an angle other than his music.

First, it is a knowledge easely taught, and quickly learned, where there is a good Master, and an apt Scoller.

2 The exercise of singing is delightfull to Nature, & good to preserue the health of Man.

3 It doth strengthen all the parts of the brest, & doth open the pipes.

4 It is a singuler good remedie for a stutting &
stamering in the speech.

5 It is the best meanes to procure a perfect pronuncia-
tion, & to make a good Orator.

6 It is the onely way to know where Nature hath
bestowed the benefit of a good voyce : which
guift is so rare, as there is not one among a
thousand, that hath it : and in many, that
excellent guift is lost, because they want Art
to expresse Nature.

7 There is not any Musicke of Instruments whatso-
ever, comparable to that which is made of the
voyces of Men, where the voices are good, and
the same well sorted and ordered.

8 The better the voyce is, the meeter it is to honour
and serue God there-with : and the voyce of
man is chiefely to be imployed to that ende.

Omnis spiritus laudet Dominum.

Since singing is so good a thing,
I wish all men would learne to sing.

After this comes the dedication in which he
makes further reference to the inaccurate copies
of his madrigals already in circulation—a further
piece of evidence, be it noted, of the vogue which
madrigal singing had at this time, at any rate in
the middle and upper ranks of society.

'To the Right Honorable Sir Christopher
Hatton knight, Lord Chancellor of England,
William Byrd wisheth long lyfe, and the same to
be most healthie and happie.

' The often desires of many my good friends,
Right honorable, and the consideration of many
untrue incorrected coppies of divers my songes
spred abroade, have beene the two causes, chiefly
moving my consent at length to put in Print the
fruits of my small skill and labors in Musicke.'
And it continues in the complimentary strain
demanded by the conventions of the time. Byrd
was then forty-five years old, but it is obvious
from this dedication that he had written English
madrigals a considerable time before this first
publication was made. Not only had faulty
copies got abroad but he had been ' at length '
persuaded by his friends to print an authoritative
edition, and some of the madrigals in this volume
occur also in a manuscript of the date 1581. That
his reputation as a musician was already great
appears from a further sentence in this dedication.
Speaking of the encouragement his patron may
give him, he says ' it shall incourage me to suffer
some other things of more depth and skill to
folow these, which being not yet finished, are of
divers expected and desired '. So this was to be a
first instalment, containing some early and some
recent work, to be followed (actually in the next
year) by a further volume of compositions yet
unfinished. He followed up the dedication to
the Lord Chancellor with an epistle to the reader
of which part has been quoted already and
other parts will be quoted in another context.
A second edition was published during the

composer's lifetime. The title-page bears no date, but the printer was still Thomas Este (spelt so).

There are thirty-five madrigals in this set: to the same year belong the two madrigals which Byrd contributed to *Musica Transalpina*, a publication which preceded his own by a few months.[1]

One of them appears as *La Virginella* in Byrd's own set with the notes fitted to an Italian text. This is a fresh-sounding setting in five parts of a verse from Ariosto and is called *The fair young virgin*, followed by a second part called *But not so soon*, in which a little phrase made out of a scale figure associated in the first madrigal with a growing rose to whom the fair young virgin is compared, re-appears in somewhat the same manner as similar themes re-appear in different sections of the Masses—a very early example of the use of the leit-motif principle.

Byrd did not use the term madrigal to describe these non-ecclesiastical compositions—his general designation for them is plain 'songs', but he classified them according to subject in this first volume, which he divided into three sections. The first ten are 'Psalms' and are settings of metrical versions of the Psalms of David. In the very first madrigal of the set we find a modern

---

[1] In his introduction Yonge speaks of 'some English songes lately set forth by a great Maister of Musicke, which for skill and sweetnes may content the most curious.' 'Lately set forth' seems to indicate that Byrd's first set appeared before *Musica Transalpina*.

chord, the augmented fifth in its first inversion, which was used by Edwards before him and Gibbons after him. More unusual for the period is the piquant chord of the Italian sixth (another augmented chord) in No. 4. There is always a danger in playing over these madrigals on the piano, which is not entirely absent when one hears them sung, of feeling this contrapuntal music as harmony; our modern ears do not easily shake off their harmonic habits, and as a consequence many of the less striking of Byrd's madrigals are in danger of seeming dull; when, however, we have thought ourselves back into the old idiom these occasional chords come with a strikingly modern effect. The madrigal in which this particular example occurs is one of the outstanding 'Psalms'. It is harmonically interesting; it contains one piece of word painting, but as there are eight stanzas of verse to one stanza of music it is just as well that the descriptive phrase is not too graphic to fit other contexts. 'How shall a young man prone to ill, cleanse his unbridled heart?' the psalm begins. 'Unbridled' suggests to Byrd a mixture of two-note and three-note figures which gives the music a wilful effect like syncopation. The chief topic of this part of the hundred and nineteenth Psalm is the blessedness of the laws of the Lord and the delight of bringing the stubborn human will into accord with them, so that there is no serious feeling of disunity if all the stanzas are sung. Byrd seems habitually to

set only the first or first two stanzas of a long poem
and then merely print the remaining words elsewhere, leaving their form and sentiment to fit the
music as best it may. Thus in No. 6, *O Lord,
who in Thy sacred tent ?* the question is asked by
making the first important cadence consist of a
tonic to dominant progression which corresponds
in effect with the rise in pitch of the voice in
asking a question, but there is no question in the
subsequent stanzas. There is a fine solid passage
towards the end of this psalm where all five voices
speak together in block harmony on the words
'the truth doth speake with singlenes' and to
give it further emphasis the time changes from
two to three pulses for a moment. The next
madrigal, No. 7 : *Help, Lord, for wasted are those
men*, which begins darkly for the two bass voices,
almost implying a reproach and certainly suggesting the desolation of the righteous, has nine stanzas.
Byrd has set the first two continuously and has
made no arrangement whereby the odd stanza
can be begun or ended. He would have known,
had he thought about it, that two goes into nine
four times and leaves one over—another piece of
evidence that careful as he was over setting his
words his interest did not go beyond those which
first evoked the music. He did not frame his
phrases to the life of the last verse, but only to
the first. The occurrence of this odd verse
suggests that singers like the composer did not
always work through to the end of long poems.

The tenth and last psalm is a comparatively superficial setting of *De profundis*. Only two verses are taken and except for an unexpected B flat in the top and bottom parts a few bars from the end which lends poignancy to the petition, the whole has a smooth plain C major-ish feeling. The opening plunge, however, is striking :

Even from the depth, un_to . . . . . thee, Lord

Below this psalm Byrd writes 'Heere endeth the Psalmes, and beginneth the Sonets and Pastorales '. This middle section of the volume contains sixteen sonnets and pastorals. The word ' pastorals ' does not appear in the full title, and its absence seems to have been responsible for a misapprehension as to Byrd's quality as a madrigal composer. Byrd, like Gibbons, undoubtedly excelled in music of the graver type, and did not, like Morley, write a large number of madrigals of a vivacious character, but it is a mistake to suppose that he was incapable of writing a madrigal of full-blooded gaiety. The numerous critics and historians who have fallen into this error need have looked no further than the second madrigal in the second section of this, his first published collection—*Though Amaryllis dance in green* (No. 12). This has been recorded for gramophone (H.M.V. E292) and is frequently sung by the English Singers, who always bring out the rueful humour of the refrain, *Hey ho, I'll love no more.* The words are typically Elizabethan, and as they cannot easily be heard when sung the first and last verses may be quoted here:

> Though Amarillis dance in green
> > Lyke Fayrie Queene,
> > And sing full clere
> Corinna can, with smiling cheer:
> Yet since their eyes make heart so sore
> > Hey ho, chil love no more.

> Love ye who list, I force him not
> > Sith God it wot;
> > The more I wayle
> The lesse my sighes and teares prevaile;
> What shall I do but say therefore
> > Hey ho, chil[1] love no more.

The intermediate verses tell of the struggle between attraction and the wounded pride that resolves to abandon love. Byrd illustrates the mental conflict by employing two rhythms—a jiggety trochiac and an even triple measure, expressed musically as compound duple time, $\frac{6}{4}$ or two dotted minims to the bar, and simple triple time, $\frac{3}{2}$ or three plain minims to the bar. The word 'dance' suggests the lively up-and-down of compound time which thenceforth stands for the allurements of Amaryllis and Corinna, while the lover fortifies his impotent resolution with the sturdy constancy of level

---

[1] Chil, i.e. I will.

minims which grow more frequent towards the end. At the beginning the two rhythms occur in alternate bars, then simultaneously in the same bar in different voice parts, and since either rhythm may be resolved into six crochets there are some ambiguous bars. Byrd was very fond of this device, and employs it again to illustrate a somewhat similar idea in *If women could be fair and never fond* (No. 17). Brahms, who was fascinated by rhythmic ingenuities, sometimes employed a similar device (e.g. in the *Song of Destiny*, though he uses a different notation and is expressing very different sentiments).

No. 16, *O you that hear this voice*, shows some of the limitations both of the madrigal form and of Byrd as a wielder of it. The words of Sir Philip Sidney are a debate pursued through nine stanzas between the advocates of a lady's voice and of her face, as to which constitutes her claim to praise and 'limitless renown'. Byrd has not made the smallest differentiation between the music of the two competitors—not even to the extent of using different voices antiphonally as he does for less pictorial reasons in the Masses. There is no repetition of words, and he just plugs rather dully, line by line, through the two stanzas which he has set. In the second part, which fits the second stanza, he has introduced rhythmic complications between the parts to indicate the swaying argument, but there is no attempt to fit the poem into a semi-dramatic frame, no moulding of the design of the whole to give point to the antithesis which is the root idea of the poem. The madrigal writers approached the problem of form in music from an elementary point of view. They had not reached the sense of key which was natural to Purcell a hundred years later, nor to the balance of keys as a means of giving unity to a composition which Bach and the classical writers developed half a century after that. They took over their form ready made from the poet, setting his words phrase by phrase with the elaboration permitted by the counterpoint of the time (imitation and the like). Byrd is not uniformly successful in reproducing the mood of a poem, but it is surprising how far he and, to an even greater extent, his junior contemporaries still following the piecemeal method convey the general feeling of the verses they set. Their imaginations were fired by single words and phrases, which they illustrated with a wealth of harmonic detail, discords, suspensions, snatches of block harmony and the like, with phrases significant of slow or quick motion and, as we have seen, with rhythmic devices. An example of the last two ways of illuminating detail may be found in *Ambitious Love* (No. 18), where an idea appears in the shape and motion of a phrase

Pro_ceed then in this des_per.ate en___ter___prise

They were not, however, indifferent to problems of form, and many later ways of giving unity to a composition are foreshadowed—repetition, recapitulation and the like ; while the older method of the canto fermo is sometimes retained. But just as they thought of harmony as single chords brought about by the movements of the parts to illustrate particular words and not as a series of progressions, and just as they used rhythm as a means of giving character to individual phrases and not as regular framework of recurring pulses on which to weave a varied pattern, so they had not evolved a form for vocal music based on long self-supporting melodies. The modern listener therefore must not expect these classical features in the madrigals of the pre-classical period, he must adjust himself to a texture of short phrases woven together with great ingenuity and skill, to a structure built up of highly polished details fitted together with a fine sense of proportion, to an easy movement propelled by many flexible and independent rhythms reinforcing each other at intervals to provide a metrical foundation to the whole, to a harmony which is often bold in its use of individual chords but which cannot from the nature of the case venture far from its base. These limitations of the style are sometimes felt in some of these early secular madrigals of Byrd more than in the similar works of Morley, Weelkes, Wilbye and the rest. *In Fields Abroad* (No. 22), for example, is a very dashing set of verses, but the music though vigorous does not do them justice. On the other hand the gay open air feeling of a summer morning such as often appears in English folk-song is happily caught in *What pleasure have great princes ?* (No. 19), which swings along on clear bright harmonies. The fragment *Although the Heathen Poets*, No. 21, with its pattering rhythm interrupted by a trochaic bar is very crisp. An even more striking change of rhythm occurs in No. 26, *The match that's made*, a homily on matrimony, where after a stanza in which under cover of curious time signatures varied rhythms are woven together, the main rhythm changes from simple to compound at the Latin refrain *pari jugo dulcis tractus* (sweet the haulage when the yoke is evenly harnessed)—so sweet that the pair skip along in a flowing ⅜ time ! There seems to be no limit to Byrd's rhythmic resource, which pours out at the slightest suggestion.

' Heere endeth the Sonets and Pastoralles, and beginneth Songes of Sadnes and Pietie '. Of these two are elegies for Sir Philip Sidney ; two might do for anthems ; one, *All as a Sea* (No. 28), is a setting of an allegory that recalls Shakespeare's Seven Ages of Man and Raleigh's *What is our Life ?* which was set by Orlando Gibbons.

> All as a sea the world no other is ;
> Ourselves are shippes stil tossed to and fro

it begins, while the second verse pursues the simile :

Our passions be the Pirats still that spoyle
  And overboard cast out our reasons straight :
The Mariners that day and night doe toyle
  Be our conceits that doe on pleasures waight ;
Pleasure, Maister, doth tirannize the ship
  And giveth vertue secretlie the nippe.

If that a Sinner's Sighs (No. 30) is a penitential
song to which Byrd's smooth but austere style is
so well fitted ; it contains a little melisma at the
end on the words ' wept most bitterly ', which
though not so chromatic recalls Bach's similar
treatment of the same words in the *St Matthew
Passion.* No. 32 is one of the best known of all
Byrd's mardigals, *Lullaby, my sweet little Baby.*
It is in two parts, of which the first is often sung
separately and has been so recorded for gramophone
(E232). This is no more than the refrain of what
is in its complete form a lullaby Christmas carol.
The whole thing is extraordinarily beautiful and
tender, showing the peculiar clean quality of
Byrd's harmony in a softened form, and along
with the other exquisite lullaby for solo voice and
strings, *My little sweet darling,* throwing a light
on Byrd's temperament, revealing beneath its
outward severity towards the big religious issues
of life a melting tenderness worthy of a woman
towards the personal appeal of a baby. In the
second part, which is not often heard, there is
some similarity in the thematic material, but at
the contemplation of the slaughter of the
innocents the music becomes more passionate and

the voices climb higher in their register. A short loud section of vigorous indignant statement follows : ' A king is borne they say, which king this king would kil '—and the corresponding passage in the subsequent verses express a similar angry sentiment—to be succeeded at once by a line of lamentation (also common to each verse) of pathetic falling phrases, ' Oh woe and wofull heavie daie, when wretches have their wil ',— pathetic rather than mournful, as the lament is set to bright D major harmony (the prevailing mode is Dorian) which turns away to allow a chord of G minor with its prominent B flat to occur on the word ' heavy '. As a whole the madrigal shows Byrd's imaginative powers at their highest, the touch is delicate, in the verse part there is the depth and restraint characteristic of his religious music, but illumined with a poetical and human radiance, while in the refrain the great man has completely unbent and shows a warm graciousness rare in his music, which again suggests a similarity with some traits in Brahms. There is a curious contemporary reference[1] to this madrigal in a letter from the Earl of Worcester, Byrd's patron, to the Earl of Shrewsbury, dated September 19, 1602 :

' We are frolic here at Court ; much dancing in the Privy Chamber of Country Dances before the Queen's Majesty, who is exceedingly pleased therewith. Irish tunes are at this time most liked ; but in winter " Lullaby," an old song of

[1] Talbot Papers; College of Heralds.

Mr. Byrd's, will be more in request as I think.'
Why 'in winter'? Perhaps by this time *Lullaby*,
which is after all a Christmas carol, had become
an established favourite.

> Why do I use my paper incke and pen
>> And call my wits to counsel what to saie ?
> Such memories were made for mortall men :
>> I speak of Saints whose names cannot decaye.
> An Angels' trump were fitted for to sound
> Their glorious death, if such on earth were found.

These words were written by Father Henry
Walpole on the martyrdom of Edmond Campion,
the Jesuit, in December, 1581,[1] a theme which
stirred another side of Byrd's imagination and
moved him to vigorous splendour such as he
showed in the great Latin motets. This madrigal
(No. 33) is recorded for gramophone along with
Come to me grief forever, which stands next to it
in the book (No. 34) (H.M.V. D711). The latter
is the first and shorter of the two ' funerall Songs
of that honorable Gent. Syr Phillip Sidney,
Knight '. It is a simple and moving elegy. The
words of the first verse are passable, but of the
other verses the simplicity degenerates into the
kind of bald doggerel which still finds its way into
the In Memoriam columns of newspapers. Byrd,
however, concentrates his attention on the first
verse, here as usual, and the nobility of *Why do
I use my paper ink and pen ?* and the simple pathos

[1] So Dr Grattan Flood in *Musical Times*, Nov., 1926.

of *Come to me grief, forever*, move him to two very different but equally fine expressions of feeling in music.

In the dedication of this 1588 set Byrd says that if it is well received he will issue some more. 'Most humbly beseeching your Lordship, that if my boldnesse heerein be faultie, my dutifull good will, and good meaning may excuse it : which if I may so fortunately perceive, it shall incourage me to suffer some other things of more depth and skill to folow these, which being not yet finished, are of divers expected and desired .'

This promise he redeemed in the following year (1589), when he published *Songs of sundrie natures, some of | gravitie, and others of myrth, fit for all compa- | nies and voyces. Lately made and composed in- | to Musick of 3. 4. 5 and 6. parts : and pub- | lished for the delight of all such as take plea- | sure in the exercise of | that Art.* In addressing once more ' the curteous Reader ' he acknowledges the good reception of the first volume and comments on the increase in the practice of madrigal singing.

The general opinion does not agree with Byrd's own estimate that the madrigals of the 1589 set are ' of more depth and skill ' than the 1588. They are however more varied, not merely in the matter of difficulty but in 'serving for all companies and voyces '. All the madrigals we have so far examined are for five voices. The Songs of Sundrie Natures are classified not according to their subject but according as they are for three, four, five or six voices. The first fourteen, which are for three voices, are however assigned in two equal portions to psalms and to secular subjects. There are sacred madrigals mixed among the remainder of the forty-seven pieces that made up the volume, including two Christmas Carols, two Easter anthems and three settings of psalms. Of the psalms the most striking is No. 6, *From depth of sin*, which begins with a downward plunge of an octave in each part, while the lowest part at a later stage makes a number of wide upward leaps including several octave jumps. It also contains an instance of the use of an inversion of the chord of the sharpened fifth. As in the former volume at the end of the section Byrd writes ' Heere endeth the seven Psalmes ', and he then proceeds to some lively three-part madrigals. The lighter texture for three voices with a frequent crossing of the parts and generally a quickening of musical interest towards the end makes the seven secular madrigals a delightful manifestation of the composer's lighter vein and the discreet gaiety that marks some of his keyboard music. No. 8, *Susanna Fair*, is a setting in three parts of the same words as Byrd had already set to five voices in his 1588 set. Most composers nowadays would find this difficult to do ;[1] when the right expression has been found

---

[1] They sometimes do it, however; Vaughan Williams has made at least two settings of *Orpheus with his lute*.

it is difficult to think of it in other terms. *The Nightingale so pleasant* (No. 9) with its little runs is very jolly and attractive ; Nos. 10 and 11 are related to each other as first and second parts ; so also are Nos. 12 and 13. *The Greedy Hawk* has a very determined duple rhythm against which syncopations in the top and long notes in the bottom part illustrate the idea of keeping at bay, while the word ' soaring ' at the end gives the composer an opportunity for weaving together some flowing phrases that overlap in a way at once pictorial and musical.

Of the four-part madrigals in this set only one is to sacred words—No. 22, *O Lord my God, let flesh and blood thy servant not subdue.* Several of the settings of typical Elizabethan poems about the boy Cupid are not specially interesting; two are in two parts, one in three. These ' parts ' are really different madrigals and in the original publication begin on a fresh page with a new illuminated initial letter, just like an entirely separate composition. The thought of the poem however is continuous and Byrd sometimes begins the second part with a phrase reminiscent in shape of something he has used in the first part. *Is Love a boy ?* (No. 15) is fanciful, the suggestion of pouting and exploiting a grievance is reflected in the descending figures of the music, and the voices throw their rhetorical questions at one another in effective imitation. But the outstanding number is *While that the sun with his beams hot* (No. 23), which is a bright pastoral on a big scale, elaborate in design and in the ingenuity of its changing rhythms. The refrain:

> Adieu love, adieu love, untrue love,
> Untrue love, untrue love, adieu love,
> Your mind is light, soon lost for new love

is dramatically conceived—which is somewhat rare in Byrd. The last 'adieu' is sung homophonically to long notes, and the lightness of the lady's mind throws off a skirmish of quavers; and in performance play of expression will make it most effective. Included among this group of four-part madrigals is a chorus for two sopranos and two altos which belongs to a Christmas carol which is placed at No. 35 in the original edition. This carol, *From Virgin's Womb this day did spring*, is for a solo voice (alto) with accompaniment for four string parts and is therefore included in the five-part group. Each could be performed separately, but Byrd intended them to go together and in performance they fit admirably. No. 35 he describes as 'A Carowle for Christmas day the quire whereof (Reioyce) beeing of 4 parts, is the xxiiii. song'. The 'carowle' is a melodious solo with a flowing accompaniment in which the treble viol has some pleasing dialogue with the singer, and works up to a spacious climax. The effect of the 'quire' coming in on high voices with brilliant runs which race along, first of all one after the other, then two and

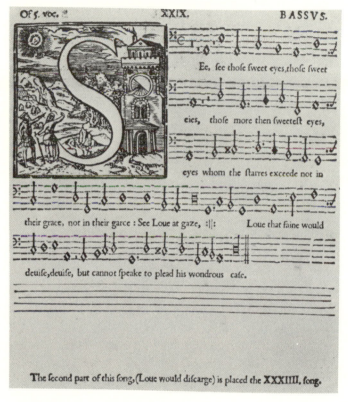

A PAGE FROM A PART-BOOK OF THE 1589 SET OF MADRIGALS

(Bodleian Library)

finally three together, makes a riot of happy sound. It is worth noticing that Byrd begins this chorus in compound pastoral rhythm like so many writers of Christmas music (e.g. Bach and Handel), and as in other carols passages often move in thirds and sixths. It cannot be a case of association that gives these features to Christmas music, it can only be that the mind of man symbolizes this Christmassy emotion in auditory images of this shape. The same features, though less marked, are to be found in the other carol chorus of this set (No. 25). Here, as also in No. 24, the rhythm of triplets is interrupted by more vigorous groups of four ; in both the triplet rhythm begins and the quadruple ends the chorus, though the internal distribution is different in the two cases. The ' carowle ' *An Earthly Tree a Heavenly Fruit it bare* (No. 40) is a duet for two sopranos with an accompaniment for four strings. Another curious separation of two connected madrigals is the placing of *See those sweet eyes*—in which Byrd makes great play with the long syllable ' eyes '— at No. 29 and *Love would discharge* to the same music at No. 34. The reason is not clear, but No. 34 is a longer poem and requires additional music. Both of these belong to the five-part group of which three madrigals may be briefly mentioned. *Penelope that longed for the sight* (No. 27) is a big madrigal that shows Byrd in a tender mood and expressing sympathetic feeling for his text in bold and characteristic harmony :

there is a striking juxtaposition of the chords of
D major and B flat major where ' I, poor wretch '
turn from the contemplation of the woes of
Penelope to my own, and there are several of the
strong false relations of which Byrd was so fond,
one specially notable occuring three bars from the
end, and the final cadence is a simple and beautiful
suspension on the word ' die '. *I thought that
Love had been a boy* (No. 32) is a very vivacious
piece to be sung at a great pace. It too contains
some striking modal harmony—a perfect triad on
the flattened seventh of the scale immediately
after a tonic chord, both in root position, and some
characteristic syncopation and cross rhythms.

Even more striking harmonic progressions are to
be found in No. 36, *If gold all burnished*, where
the Shakespearian richness of language leads the
composer by quick modulations from F major
through C to D to A, to return as rapidly through
D minor to the prevailing tonality. It seems
right to speak of keys and modulations rather
than modes in this madrigal, though the changes of
key are more abrupt than the classical composers
would have tolerated. The parts sing a good deal
homophonically and the effect is neat.

The six-part group is composed mainly of big settings of sacred words, which though ostensibly written for domestic use make excellent anthems. Their smooth style suggests the rolling echoes of a cathedral, and evokes that unique emotion compounded of antiquity, dispassionate contemplation and the unity of the human race, which we sometimes call the communion of saints. This applies not only to the settings of Scriptural words but to the moral sentiments of *If in thine heart* (No. 44), which is written for an odd combination of voices (soprano, alto, three tenors and a bass). No. 41, *What made thee Hob forsake the plow?* ; ' A Dialogue between two Shepherds,' reveals Byrd in quite a new humour. Two shepherds sing question and answer to one another to a gruff accompaniment of three tenor viols and one bass viol. The voice parts are assigned to the ' superius ' and 'sextus ' part books (i.e. the two highest) and are in the soprano clef, so that perhaps Byrd imagined them as shepherd boys in the first pangs of calf-love. But the words do not read quite like that, and so we may be justified artistically in departing from Byrd's text to the extent of assigning the voice parts to men and singing them an octave lower. The voices bring out the humour of the words— the sharp question and the soft answer ; the repartee is rapid (a quick tempo in triple time), and the singers finish with a brief duet to ' yet love I must, or else I die '. The whole is

humorously conceived and dramatically executed.
Another madrigal of light and delightful character
is *And think ye nymphs* (No. 42) for five voices,
with a second part for six voices, *Love is a fit
of pleasure* ; the air of both is of mocking gaiety,
almost cheekiness. The last two madrigals in
the volume are Easter carols for voices and viols
similar to the Christmas carols we have already
examined, though the distribution of what is
played and what is sung is different. The lower
strings begin, then the two upper voices enter ;
when the emphatic words ' Death from henceforth ' are reached all six voices sing together, and
the viols undoubtedly continued to play, doubling
the voice parts. The words of *Christ is Risen*,
the second part so-called, are from 1 Corinthians
xv 20-22, and provide Byrd with ample opportunity
for the expression of the religious feeling which
meant so much to him, and his vivid, almost
dramatic, treatment may be enhanced in performance by a judicious use of string and organ
accompaniment. The change in the music from
' For as in Adam all die ' to ' even so in Christ
all men shall be restored ' is as marked as in
Messiah : the first is homophonic, slow and quiet,
the second is in hurried imitations running over
one another with eagerness and life. The second
phrase ' So by Christ ' is reiterated with different
treatment, slower, solider, allowing the organ to
come in with good effect and working up gradually
to the end, to be followed by a quiet Amen of

gratitude. It is usually admitted that Byrd's Latin church music is his noblest work, but this anthem, madrigal or 'carowle' is a sufficient answer in itself to anyone who would claim that Byrd's other sacred music was written in a perfunctory professional way, untouched by real religious feeling.

More than twenty years elapsed before Byrd published his third and last set of madrigals. In 1610 came the second edition of the first book of *Gradualia*, in which Byrd already speaks of his swan song; in 1611 appeared the 'ultimum vale' (last farewell)—his own description of *Psalmes Songs and | Sonnets : some solemne others | joyfull framed to the life of the | Words : Fit for Voyces or Viols | of* 3, 4, 5 *and* 6 *Parts.* It is dedicated to Francis, Earl of Cumberland, to whom the composer says : 'The Naturall inclination and loue to the Art of *Musicke*, wherein I have spent the better part of mine age, have beene so powerfull in me, that even in my old yeares which are desirous of rest, I cannot containe myselfe from taking some paines therein: especially when I cast mine eyes upon such worthy lovers and Patrons of that facultie, as your Lordship hath alwayes beene, and is. . . . These are like to be my last Travailes in this kind, and your Lordship my last Patron : who in that respect

—*ut esse Phoebi dulcius lumen solet
iam iam cadentis :*[1]

As Apollo's ray is sweeter yet the nearer 'tis to setting.

must esteeme the more of them, and of their Author, who will alwayes remayne

> *Your lordships in all true affection at command, William Byrd.*

His introduction is addressed ' to all true lovers of Musicke ', to whom ' W. Byrd wisheth all true happinesse both temporall and eternall '. He points out that first hearings are no test of the final pleasure to be obtained from a song any more than first performances are likely to do justice to the composer's intentions.

' Being exited by your kinde acceptance of my former travailes in Musicke. I am thereby much incouraged to commend to you these my last labours, for myne *ultimum vale*. Wherein I hope you shall finde Musicke to content every humour : either melancholy, merry, or mixt of both.

' Only this I desire : that you will be but as carefull to heare them well expressed, as I have been in the Composing and correcting of them. Otherwise the best song that ever was made will seeme harsh and unpleasant, for that the well expressing of them, either by Voyces, or Instruments, is the life of our labours, which is seldome or never well performed at the first singing or playing. Besides a song that is well and artificially made cannot be well perceived nor understood at the first hearing, but the oftner you shall heare it, the better cause of liking you will discover : and commonly that Song is best esteemed with which our eares are most acquainted.

As I have done my best endeavour to give you content, so I beseech you satisfie my desire in hearing them well expressed: and then I doubt not, for *Art* and *Ayre* both of skilfull and ignorant they will deserve liking. *Vale*

Thine W. Byrd.

The volume contains thirty-two numbers— eight each to three, four, five and six voices. They are even more varied in character than the 1589 set. Two pieces are for instruments, the fantasia in four parts, a grave little piece of string music similar in construction to a madrigal, and the big six-part fantasia already examined. There are two carols, and ten psalms distributed through the volume, and in several madrigals Byrd carries a stage further his experiments in mixing string and voices ; the last two numbers are in fact soprano solos with string quintet accompaniment. Byrd reprinted in this set his four-part setting of *This sweet and merry month of May* which he had contributed to Thomas Watson's *First set of Italian Madrigals Englished* in 1590. He also wrote a six-part setting of the same words for the same volume, but fails to reprint that in 1611 with as little reason as he reprints the four-part setting. Dr Fellowes, however, includes it at the end of his recent edition, for which we may be glad, as it is a fine work in Byrd's most joyous style—'composed after the Italian vaine' is Thomas Watson's recommendation of these ' two excellent Madri- gals '. The six-part setting has been recorded for gramophone (H.M.V. E292). It is difficult when hearing this madrigal to remember that it was not composed for *The Triumphs of Oriana*. This was a collection of madrigals in praise of Queen Elizabeth edited by Thomas Morley and published in 1601. Most of the great composers of the day contributed, but for some unexplained reason no madrigal of Byrd's appears among the twenty-five. Dr. Walker[1] suggests that Byrd's style being notorious for its " gravity and piety " Morley hesitated to ask him for something that was to be at once secular and exuberant. But *This sweet and merry month* seems in itself a sufficient answer to this objection. There is great rhythmic variety, and the time signature changes ₵ to $\frac{3}{4}$, $\frac{6}{8}$ and $\frac{3}{2}$ as different ideas (' merry ', ' wanton ', ' sing ', ' play ', ' pleasure ', and ' O beauteous Queen ') demand expression. One very delightful touch is the way in which the male voices as it were throw up their hats on the words ' and greet Eliza '. The four-part setting reproduces the same rhythmic features.

The three-part madrigals in this volume are settings of words that exhort to worldly wisdom, often with references to animals like the eagle and the ant that give them an Æsopian flavour. This does not make for very inspired music, and the best of the eight is *Sing ye to our Lord*, which is more spontaneous, and being written for four high voices is bright in effect. It may be compared

[1] *History of Music in England*, p. 90.

with the anthem *Sing joyfully* (six parts) and *Sing
we merrily unto God* (in five parts, No. 20 and 21
in this set). There is a general similarity of
treatment by which the voices first toss the joyful
running phrases to one another and then combine
two at a time in thirds and sixths. In the two
larger works, which are settings of verses from the
eighty-first Psalm, Byrd sets the words ' Blow the
trumpet in the new moon ' with reiterations of a
single chord, the voices surging up and down the
natural harmonics like a bugle call. *Sing we
merrily* leads off with a theme made of an ascending
scale of an octave, and the thrumming of harps is
represented by repeated quavers in the lowest
part. It is noteworthy that these picturesque
details, which Byrd uses pretty freely, never upset
the balance of the work as a whole, but give to it
vigour or distinction. The eight four-part
madrigals contain several examples of Byrd in a
sportive mood, which shows the influence of his
pupil Morley, who by this time had published
half a dozen volumes and been dead eight years.
There are distinct traces of Morley's gay manner
in *Awake mine eyes* and *Come jolly swains* (Nos.
12 and 13). In *Come woeful Orpheus* No. 19,
one of the outstanding songs of the set, Byrd
shows unusual boldness even for him in the use of
chromatic harmony to give suitable expression to
the words ' Of sourest sharps and uncouth flats
make choice '. Nos. 25 and 28 (*Have mercy upon
me* and *O God that guides the cheerful sun*) are

compositions comparable both in form and scale to the anthems which he wrote 'with verses to the organ'. No. 25 is of a smooth and devotional character and contains a good deal of soprano solo, and the instructions 'versus' and 'chorus' are cued in—strings play throughout, doubling the voice parts as is usual in madrigals of this type when words are written beneath the music. No. 28 is described as a "Carroll for New-yeares day"—Byrd is no more consistent in his spelling, it may be noted, than other great men of the period. It is a big joyous thing, though the solo voice only leaves a little to the chorus to do ; the entry of the chorus however is effective and finishes the carol with a fine 'Amen' very characteristic of the composer. No. 26 is the six-part fantasia for strings. No. 27 is the 'carroll' for Christmas Day, *This day Christ was born* (H.M.V. E305) recorded by the English Singers ; C1334 recorded in the new electrical process by the choir of York Minster), one of the most splendid things in all Byrd's work, scored for two high sopranos, two altos, a tenor and a bass, a combination of high voices that gives an airiness, elation and brilliancy that suggests the angelic host. Vigour and buoyancy is obtained by the voices leading each other in imitation, and by change of rhythm ; two passages may specially be remarked—the broadening out on the word 'saying' introduced by the juxtaposition of a chord of E major to a chord of C, and the

crisp shouts of 'Alleluia' obtained by bringing the top parts on to the last syllable one
beat before the rest, but taking all off together.
This madrigal ought to appear in every programme of Christmas music that has any
pretensions to include something more than 'old
favourites'. *Praise our Lord all ye Gentiles* (No.
29) and *Turn our Captivity* (No. 30), both big
sacred madrigals, have also been recorded for
gramophone (H.M.V. D710 and 711). *Praise our
Lord* expresses serene confidence rather than great
exaltation ; it seems rather to voice Byrd's personal
attitude to his faith than to be a setting of any
particular words ; in it we seem to get a glimpse
of the man as well as his religion, and as with
Byrd religion was the core of his life, this one
madrigal of his old age gives not perhaps a complete
portrait of him, but a characteristic picture of him
in a typical frame of mind. Fortunately it is
one of the few works of his, outside the two or
three really well-known compositions, that is
occasionally to be heard nowadays. *Turn our
Captivity* shows at once the strength and the
weakness of the Elizabethan method of setting
words. Music by itself has considerable power
of conveying complex emotions, and when allied
with words it can express them with depth and
precision ; further it can reveal the strength of
them and show them in process of changing into
other emotions as they do in life. Byrd is
particularly happy (so it would seem) in the

expression of the rather sad kind of emotion of the 126th Psalm. When he comes to the words 'They that sow in tears' he gives to different voices a drooping phrase and a halting phrase; before these have finished he brings in a lower voice with a strong upward thrusting phrase ('shall reap in joyfulness') which gradually changes the character of the music until he reaches 'they shall come with jollity', where he breaks into a new rhythm with the voices singing all together. This break is so marked as to sound slightly ludicrous. Byrd is here employing inaptly a device which in lighter madrigals like *Though Amaryllis dance in green* is most effective, but with these words the result is so incongruous that we may criticize it even while we bear in mind that criticism should be historical and that this was a regular feature of 'underlaying' words of this period. The last two numbers in the volume are both solo songs for soprano with string accompaniment. The vogue of the solo voice was beginning in earnest by the time Byrd published these songs in madrigal form. John Dowland in England and Claudio Monteverde in Italy had in different ways begun to isolate a single vocal line from its fellows, which were henceforth until the time of Wagner and Wolf to be depressed to the position of accompaniment. Both the lute accompaniment to Dowland's ayres and the orchestral support with which Monteverde sustained his recitative were leading away from the contrapuntal style altogether.

Byrd never went as far as this, but as early as 1581 he had written a solo song *My little sweet darling*[1] in which the string accompaniment is quite independent, not cast in the usual contrapuntal idiom of imitative phrases, but going its own instrumental way while observing a proper deference to the supremacy of the voice. This cradle song, full of tenderness and feminine intimacy, with a touch of quaintness in the line 'in beauty surpassing the princes of Troy' and a delicate lilt, is not only a masterpiece but has some claim to be the earliest art song in the history of music. Claims of this sort cannot be fully substantiated, because folk song, troubador song and the early Tudor attempts at secular song (which are written however for more than one voice) show a line of development leading up to this innovation. But Caccini and the English lutenist writers usually have the credit for being the first composers of songs as we now understand the form, i.e., a setting of words for a solo voice with an independent instrumental accompaniment. The 1588 madrigals which Byrd says were 'originally made for instruments to expresse the harmonie, and one voyce to pronounce the dittie' do not correspond to this definition, but *My little sweet darling* certainly does, and it is at any rate fifteen years older than those of the English composers or the Italian. But if it is in

---

[1] Published by Staines and Bell for 1s. The original is in a Christ Church MS. dated 1581.

effect the first *lied* it seems unlikely that it was in intention, for Byrd was not here carrying out a deliberate experiment. He was merely doing in a more elaborate and finished manner what seems to have been done by his predecessors at the Chapel Royal. Choir boys, as we have already found, were chosen not only for their voices, but for their appearance in order that they might be useful for dramatic as well as musical purposes. The Chapel choir apparently entertained its royal masters by dramatic entertainments of the mixed revue type which has always been favoured in this country, up till the year 1553, when Mary came to the throne, after which time the Gentlemen of the Chapel no longer appeared as actors, though the boys continued to do so until 1585. In the early days songs were inserted into the plays without much regard for their dramatic significance, but Richard Edwards contrived to bring in his songs to heighten the effect at a climax, introducing for example a lament at the death of the hero or heroine. *O Death rock me asleep* for soprano and strings, which is sometimes attributed to Anne Boleyn and is quoted by Pistol in II Henry IV, II 4, is an example of one of these death songs. Byrd's cradle song is possibly a piece of incidental music in one of these choir-boy plays.[1]

That Byrd occasionally wrote songs for the

[1] For choir boy plays see *Musical Association Proceedings*, 1914, paper by G. E. P. Arkwright.

stage is proved by the song which he wrote for the production of a Latin play at St. John's College, Cambridge, in 1579.[1] It is usually regarded as a three-part song,[2] but it is impossible to make any sense out of it. " Triplex " was the name often used for the soprano part-book of a set, and this song is written in the mezzo-soprano clef with a " medius " or second part in the soprano clef which looks like a refrain. But what the third part was or how it fitted is a puzzle which cannot be unravelled from the present text.

The play was *Ricardus III* by Thomas Legge of Caius, who in all probability provided Latin entertainment for a royal visit and achieved some success in this dramatic field. The words of the song occur at the end of the first act ; after an epilogue a penitential procession is formed, so that possibly this is the music of a processional hymn, though there are no directions that it is to be sung at this point. Jane Shore was mistress of Edward IV, and on his death was accused of sorcery and of being a harlot. Beside being imprisoned she was compelled to undergo penance, and this piece of incidental music is a prayer for delivery from the evils of adultery.

[1] Stafford Smith, *Musica Antiqua*, assigns it to a play by Henry Lacy in 1586. This, however, is a copy, and may be found in the British Museum, Harleyan Collection, no. 6926. The reference number of the original is Harley 2412.

[2] Both by Mr. Barclay Squire, Grove's Dictionary, 3rd edition, and Stafford Smith, who prints the music in his *Musica Antiqua*.

S. Triplex

Pre _ ces De _ o fun _ da _ mus fun _ da _ mus o _ re sup _ pli _ ces ne sit no _ ta pol _ lu _ ta mens a _ dul _ te _ ra ne sit no _ ta pol _ lu _ ta me _ ns a _ dul _ te _ ra mens a _ dul _ te _ ra

1. _ Fi _ dem tu _ e _ re con _ ju _ gum lec _ tum que pro _ bo lib _ e _ ra de _ fen _ de de _ fen _ de pri _ va _ tos tho _ ros fur _ ti _ va ne le _ dat ve _ nus

2. _ Quae _ cun _ que fac _ ti poe _ ni _ tet pur _ ga so _ lu _ tum cri _ mi _ ne ex _ em _ pla ex _ em _ pla fa _ vent post _ er _ os fur _ ti _ va ne foe _

M.r Bird

Medius _ dat ve _ nus

S.

Pre _ ces De _ o Pre _ ces De _ o

192

THE SHEWE OF THE PROCESSION
A Tipstaffe,
Shore's Wife, in her petticote having a taper burninge
in her hand,
The Verger,
Queristers,
Singinge men,
Prebendaries,
The Bishope of London,
Citizens.

Whether this hymn of Byrd's was sung during
the procession or not, a stage direction at the end
of the play explicitly requires ' . . . and the
song sung which is at the end of this book.
Preces Deo.'

193

CHAPTER VII

WM. BYRD : THE MAN, HIS LIFE AND HIS ACHIEVEMENTS

SUCH then was the work which Byrd accomplished in the course of a long life at one of the most vital periods of English history. What sort of a man was it who produced this work ? The known facts of his life are scanty for a full biography; the only extant portrait of him is of doubtful authenticity; to deduce the personality of an artist from his art is fraught with danger of fantastic error, yet this is the only source on which we can draw copiously for material. A certain number of episodes in his career seem both to confirm and to supplement the estimate of the man which gradually forms itself in the mind after an investigation of the music such as we have pursued in the last four chapters, and the out-standing events of his career are known upon good evidence.

He was born in Lincolnshire in 1543. We know this date from his will, signed on November 15th, 1622, which begins : ' In the name of the most glorious and undevided Trinitye Father sonne holy Gost three distinct persons and one eternall God Amen I William Byrd of Stondon Place in the pish of Stondon in the Countye of Essex gentleman doe now in the 80th yeare of myne age but through ye goodnes of God beeinge of good health and pfect memory make and ordayne this for my last will and Testament.'[1] He received his musical education from the great Thomas Tallis. The authority for this is Anthony Wood the antiquary, who says he was ' bred up to musick under Thomas Tallis '. This raises the questions How ? and Where ? For Tallis was in London at the Chapel Royal and Byrd presumably at his home in Lincolnshire. It has been conjectured from this and other evidence, which finds no confirmation in the documents of the cathedral, that Byrd was a chorister at St. Paul's in 1554 when the choir petitioned for certain emoluments due to them ; but the petition cannot be found, and when the emoluments were paid the name of William Byrd does not occur among the recipients, and Anthony Wood's words might be stretched to cover the early days of Byrd's association with Tallis at the Chapel Royal. So we cannot be certain whether he spent any of his youth in London. It is certain however that he was in Lincoln in 1563, for he was appointed organist of the cathedral on February 27th. This is the first authenticated fact of his career—he was a cathedral organist at the age of twenty. Five

---

[1] The complete text of the will was reprinted in *The Musician* of June 2nd, 1897, and is quoted by Dr Fellowes in his monograph published by the Clarendon Press, 1923.

years later he married (on September 14th) Juliana Birley, sometimes called Ellen, who a year later (November 18th, 1569) bore him a son, Christopher. On February 22, 1570, he was elected a Gentleman of the Chapel Royal, to take the place of Robert Parsons who had been drowned in the Trent at Newark a month before, but he does not seem to have gone permanently to London until 1572, for it was only on December 7th of that year that Thomas Butler was appointed to succeed him at Lincoln ' on ye nomination and commendation of Mr William Byrd ', and his third child Elizabeth was baptized there on January 20th, 1572. Byrd was now settled in the forefront of his profession early in life, and the chief landmarks of his career are the publications of his various works. In about 1593 he became a country gentleman, moving from Harlington in Middlesex to Stondon Place, a farm of 200 acres near Ongar in Essex. The coat of arms which he assumed was sanctioned by the Herald's Visitation of Essex in 1634, when his grandson, Thomas Byrd, was the occupant of the property; and the pedigree was then officially recorded. In this, however, the composer's parentage is unfortunately not stated, and it is impossible to do more than conjecture that he was the son of Henry Byrde,[1] a former mayor of Newcastle, who

---

[1] Dr Grattan Flood inclines to the view that the Thomas Byrd of Edward VI's chapel (see above) was the composer's father. (*Musical Times*, Nov., 1926.)

died at Lincoln in 1512. This is no more than a conjecture, because Bird was a common name in these parts at the time. During the latter part of his life Byrd enjoyed the patronage and the protection of many of the greatest noblemen of the land, and his position was such that he was able to realize his ambition of founding a county family.

This does not sound a very eventful chronicle, but his unswerving allegiance to the Catholic faith and a strong streak of tenacity in his character which led him into frequent litigation interspersed the tranquil business of writing music with more exciting episodes. Father William Weston, whose description of the clandestine celebration of the old Catholic rites has already been quoted (*supra* C. III, p. 81), in the same passage says : ' We met there [i.e. at the house of Mr Bold in Berkshire] also Mr Byrd, the most celebrated musician and organist of the English nation, who had been formerly in the Queen's Chapel, and held in the highest estimation ; but for his religion he sacrificed everything, both his office and the Court and all those hopes which are nurtured by such persons as pretend to similar places in the dwellings of princes, as steps towards the increasing of their fortunes.' This is a gross over-statement of the amount of persecution suffered by Byrd for the sake of his religion, and the cheque book of the Chapel Royal lends no support to the allegation that Byrd forfeited his place there ; his name appears constantly until 1603, when he received an allowance for mourning livery, and he was present at the coronation of James I. It is possible that by this time he had ceased to be an active member of the choir, though he is mentioned in 1618 in the time of Orlando Gibbons's organistship as a Gentleman, and he received livery for the funeral of Queen Anne, the wife of James I, who died on March 2nd, 1619.[1] But he and his family were frequently summoned at the Sessions as recusants ' for not going to church, chapel or any usual place of common prayer '. The names of ' Juliana Birde wife of William Byrde ' and John Reason a servant of Byrd's, appear in the Sessions Rolls of Middlesex under two or three dates in every year from 1581 to 1586, and as early as 1577 ' the wife of William Byrde, one of the Gentlemen of her Majesty's Chapel ' is mentioned in Bishop Aylmer's list of recusants. On October 7th, 1586 Byrd himself was indicted and on April 7th ,1592, he is indicted with the other two. His work was valued too highly at Court for him to suffer serious molestation, but the troubles of adherents to the Catholic faith are reflected in the sorrowful tone of much of the Latin Church music, and these encounters with the law must have caused him a good deal of annoyance. There is for instance an entry dated August 21st, 1586, in a list of houses to be searched : ' Mr Byrd's house in Harmansworth or

[1] *Lord Chamberlain's Accounts. Vol.* 556.

Craneford' (villages near Harlington). The pleasures of being kept under observation appear in another state paper of January 26th, 1583-4. In ' an inventory of the books and other Popish relics found in Mr Hampden's house of Stocke in the county of Bucks' there is ' an old printed song-book, which was sent unto Carleton, as appeared by a letter sent therewithal, and one other letter sent unto Mr Fytton from one Mr Byrd of the Queen's Majesty's Chapel.' It would be interesting to know what that song-book was —perhaps a copy of Thomas Wythorne's *Songes*, but more likely a volume of Italian madrigals. That he was a marked man appears in two other entries in the *Domestic State Papers of Elizabeth* : in a list of ' places where certain recusants remain in and about London' occurs William Byrd of the Chapel, at his house in the parish of Harlington in the county of Middlesex ; and in another place among 'the names of . . . suche as are relievers of papistes and conveyers of money and other thinges unto them beyonde the Seas' is ' Mr Byrde, at Mr. Lester his house, over against St Dunstan's or at the Lord Padgettes house at Drayton. The messenger is to tell him things which he will well like', which is presumably a piece of grim irony. The same kind of petty persecution followed him to Essex, since we find among the *Proceedings of the Court of Archdeaconry of Essex* an entry dated May 11th, 1605 : ' [Parish of] Standen Massie [contra] Willielmum

Byrd et Elenam ejus uxorem. Praestantur for Popish recusants. He is a gentleman of [the] King's Majesty's Chapel, and as the minister and churchwardens do hear, the said William Byrd, with the assistance of one Gabriel Colford, who is now at Antwerp, hath been the chief and principal seducer of John Wright, son and heir of John Wright of Kelvedon, in Essex, Gentleman, and of Anne Wright, the daughter of the said John Wright the elder ; and the said Ellen Byrd, as it is reported, and as her servants have confessed, hath appointed business on the Sabbath days for her servants, of purpose to keep them from church ; and hath also done her best endeavour to seduce Thoda Pigbone, her now maid-servant, to draw her to Popery, as the maid hath confessed ; and besides, hath drawn her maid-servants from time to time these seven years from coming to church ; and the said Ellen refuseth conference ; and the minister and churchwardens have not as yet spoke with the said William Byrd, because he is from home ', etc.

These minor encounters with the law did not deter him, however, from prosecuting various lawsuits of his own. It cost him the efforts of fifteen years to establish himself in the tenure of the Stondon property, but long before this he had been involved in litigation over an earlier attempt to become a landed proprietor. About 1574 he had acquired from the Earl of Oxford a thirty-one-year lease of the manor of Battles Hall in Stapleford, Essex, to take effect at the death of a certain Aubrey Ware or his wife. When this happened a few years later (1582 is the date conjectured by Mr Barclay Squire) Byrd was unable to take up his tenure, and in the lawsuit which followed he lost his case. There is an entry in the State Papers of Elizabeth's reign headed 'Statement of the practices by which D. Lewin obtained the lease of the Manor of Battylshall, to the detriment of Wm. Byrde, assignment to Anth. Luther.' Undeterred by this failure and undismayed by his continual collisions with the powers of the law in Middlesex, where he continued to live, he was engaged a few years later in a suit, of which the purpose is unknown, with one of the Fettiplaces, a prominent Berkshire family, Byrd's antagonist being the Sheriff of that county. Byrd had apparently been unlucky again in his legal enterprises, this time through a technical flaw, and we find no less influential a person than Lord Howard of Effingham writing to the court on his behalf. The State Paper under date June 10th, 1591, reads as follows :

> Lord Admiral Howard to Dr. Aubrey, Mr. Herbert
> and other Masters of Requests.
> I have heretofore written you touching a cause between William Byrde, Her Majesty's servant, complainant, and Basil Fetiplace, defendant, which being heard before you, by reason of two words left out of complainant's bill, he was driven to commence his suit again, to his no small charge. Now as the

cause, after many delays, is shortly appointed to be heard, I earnestly desire you to show Byrde all lawful favour.[1]

A good many years later when his hands were already full with the disputes over the Stondon property he took up with zest a further suit. In this, however, he was not the aggressor. The previous tenant of Stondon Place, Lawrence Hollingworth, had ' injuriously ' blocked a right of way, following a previous occupant, one Osborne Foster, who first put a fence across it about 1550. In 1596 a new rector (the Rev. John Nobbs) came to the parish, took up the matter with Byrd, who was now the occupant, and indicted him for ' stopping upp the way against the Kyng's leige people '. Byrd seems to have had the support of the squire and after a long dispute the two took the offensive and sued Nobbs at Brentwood in 1604 as a defendant. The public apparently did not back up its champion, and as the way had been closed for so long, " no man having demanded or challenged " it, the sense of grievance had evaporated and the verdict seems to have gone in favour of the plaintiffs. Nobbs too appears to have been a litigious person who is described as ' fitter to have made a lawyer than a minister'.[2]

These were all minor affairs compared with his

---

[1] *Calendar of Domestic State Papers of Elizabeth.* Addenda XXXII, 17, dated June 10th, 1591.

[2] *Exchequer Depositions,* 2 *Jas.* 1.

dispute with the Shelley family. In 1586 William Shelley, who had already for six years been in and out of prison as a papist, was brought to trial on a much graver charge, 'for that on the 15th September 25 Elizabeth (i.e. 1583), he imagined and compassed the deposition and death of the Queen, and the subversion of the established religion and government of the country.'[1] He pleaded guilty and was condemned to death. He was respited, however, and died a natural death in 1597, but his estates, including Stondon Place, were all confiscated to the Crown. It was not much more than a farm of about 200 acres in those days, and it was occupied by the Hollingworths who had it on a twenty-one-year lease from William Shelley. The two Hollingworths, Laurence and William, divided the property. Laurence soon after let his share to one Dyonice Lolly for ten years. On the death of Laurence, William bought back the other share and became tenant (from the Crown) of the whole, though Lolly continued to occupy part of it. 'The said William Hollingworth did mortgage his lease and interest unto one William Chambers, gent., and afterwards (1593) William Hollingworth and

---

[1] He was committed to the Fleet on August 13th, 1580, as a result of the countermeasures taken against the Jesuit invasion of Parsons and Campion. He was allowed periods of freedom on parole, and during one of them in 1583 he conferred at Petworth with Charles Paget, then on a visit from the Continent to the Earl of Northumberland, who was considering the possibilities of a second insurrection in favour of Mary Queen of Scots. Northumberland committed suicide, and Shelley was implicated and brought to trial. See Howell's *State Trials* 27 Elizabeth.

William Chambers did, for £300 paid them by William Byrde, sell and assign to him the said farm and all their interest in it.' Lolly continued to dwell there but his lease was defective, for after paying rent to his new landlord for a couple of years he went so far as deliberately ' to extinguish or detain his rent ' on the ground that Byrd had taken from him ' certain houses and roomes ' which his lease from the Hollingworths secured to him. Byrd promptly sued him and got a decision from the Court of Chancery in his own favour. He did not immediately eject Lolly however, who, through the intervention of a neighbour, was allowed to stay out the remainder of his lease which expired ' at the feaste of St Michael, 1597 '. Byrd meantime however had further secured his own title to the property by obtaining a crown lease. The queen granted him the property which is described in the deed as ' part of her Majestie's inheritance, parcel of the possessions of William Shelley, attainted and convicted of high treason ', for the lives of his children, Christopher, Elizabeth and Rachel.

But even now Byrd was not allowed to remain in undisputed possession, for Mrs Shelley on the death of her husband in 1597 made representations to the queen that the estate was part of her marriage jointure. Elizabeth was now willing so far to remit punishment of the family as to allow her to receive the rents of the estate, but not to go and live on it. On the accession of

King James she renewed her application ; and for a consideration of £10,000 and a compensation of £1,000 to Lord Effingham, who had applied for a grant of the estates, she regained possession, but to her diasppointment not the occupancy. Having paid this enormous sum she not unnaturally thought she had a right to do what she liked with her own. Byrd however thought otherwise, and refused to vacate at her notice to leave. He put his case to the King and got his support in the following document :

' Jan. 24th, 1604. The King to Mrs. Jane Shelley.

We lately upon your suit delivered you your jointure lands, being our inheritance, which the late queen refused to do. But you use our said grant contrary to our meaning to the undoing of our servant, William Bird, Gentleman of our Chapel. He took leases of your farm and woods of Stondon Place, in the County of Essex, now parcel of your jointure, from the late queen for three of his children's lives, paid fines and bestowed great charges on the house and barns, paid his rent ever since the death of your husband, and deserved well of you. Yet notwithstanding you go about to thrust him out of his possessions to his present undoing, having no other house, and to the great danger of his children's future estate. For staying of which your hard course, neither your own conscience, nor our benignity towards you, nor the decree of our Exchequer Chamber yet in force, nor the letters of our Privy Council, nor any reasonable composition offered you by our said servant, move you. Being a woman of great living and no charge, and having many better houses than his, we marvel that in those lands which you so lately received from us, and which are our inheritance, you offer so hard measure to our servant. Whereupon we require you to permit him to enjoy the said farm and woods, and give no cause hereafter for complaint.'

So that was that. But still she had not said her last word. In 1608 she petitioned the Earl of Salisbury that she might be ' restored to the possession of her house, Stondon Place, withheld from her by Wm. Byrde '. The full text of the petition which is to be found among the State Papers of the year,[1] and of the eight " grievances " with which she supported it is as follows :

' To the right honorable the Erle of Salisbury
　　High Treasurer of England,
　　　　The humble petition of Jane Shelley.

Your sup^t having in all dutifull respectfulnes receaved your Lo^{ps} pleasure by her Solicitor touching Bird's continuing in her house at Stondon, who no doubt by his claims hath gone about to incense your Lo^p against her, as he hath done some other great personages, suggesting unto their honors that your Sup^t intended to take away his living without any just cause or title thereunto.

Nowe for that it may appeare unto your honor howe injuriouslie the said Bird hath delt with your Sup^t for these twelve years space, and what small or no favour he deserveth of your Sup^t she humblie prayeth your Lo^p would vouchsafe the reading of the annexed. And for that for your Sup^t being aged threescore and some years hath no other house or place of habitation near the

[1] *Exchequer Decrees and Orders,* 7 Jas. I.

Citty of London wherein to rest herself in this her period of life, save onely ye said place of Stondon.

She most humblie prayeth That with the good likeing of yor hono^r she may quickly have & enjoy the same not doubting but that your Lo^p in your grave wisdome will putt difference between the Landlord & Tenante, to the end it may appeare unto your hon^r with what submissiveness & duetye she entertayneth your Lo^p mocon.'

The Earl of Salisbury's endorsement follows:

'27 October 1608.

This matter hath bene depending in Court and therefore lett her represent unto the Barons that which she hath here delivered unto me, who are better acquainted with the whole proceedings than I am, and will take some leysure to heare her complaint for I have none.

R. Salisbury.

Mrs. Shelley grievances against William Byrde.

(1) That Bird being in quiet possession of Stondon place began a suit against your Sup^t in the Exchequer Chamber tenne yeares since, and the same pursued her sithence in his wief's & childrens names, praying thereby that the Court would order her to ratifie his lease, which he had from her late Matie for three lives.

(2) Not prevailing herein, he thereupon stirred upp all the late Queen's patentees which held any part of her jointure lands, & did combyine himself with them to mainteyne severall suits against her for the same, which contynued about eight years, and procured her rents to be sequestered, and hath caused her to expend at least 1000^{li} in defence of her title.

(3) Sʳ Thomas ffludd, Mr Churchyard & the rest of the Queene's patentees upon notice of his highness letters patents granted unto your Supᵗ for enjoying of her lands did surcease their suits and all submitted themselves, saving the said Bird and one Petiver, who being encouraged by the said Bird did a long tyme continue obstinate untill of late he likewise submitted himself. ffor which the said Bird did give him vile and bitter words for doing the same.

(4) He hath likewise practised to disgrace her with divers her honorable friends and others of great quallite pʳsuading them that she was a woman of no good conscience and that she was about to put him out of his living without any just cause or title thereunto.

(5) And being told by your Supᵗˢ Counsell in her presence that he had no right to the said living, hee both then and at other tymes before her said that yf he could not hould it by right, he would holde it by might, which course he hath pursued ever since.

(6) The said Bird hath cutt downe great store of tymber Trees worth one hundred marks growing in the grounds belonging to the said place, hath felled all the underwoods worth 100ˡⁱ & made therein greate spoile and greater would have made had not the hoᵇˡᵉ Court of Exchequer taken order to the contrary.

(7) The lands in question are yearely worth 100£ for the which he hath onely paid 40 marks ꝑ an for syx yeares or thereabouts. But since the said letters patents, which beare date the ffyst (*sic*)

208

day of September in the ffirst yeare of his highnes Raigne, he hath paid nothing at all: howbeit by the said Letters patents she was to receave the meane profytte thereof ever since the death of her husband who died about vii yeares since.

(8) That for wante of this house your Sup^t was inforced in this last plague to remove from Towne to Towne, from whence being driven by reason of the plague there, she was at the last constrayned to lye at a tenants house of hers, neare Colchester far unfitting for her to her great disgrace and to the great hurt of your Sup^t, being unable in respect of her age to travaile upp and downe the country.

All wch notwithstanding in her bounden duty to yor hono^r and with a reverend respect to yor Lo^{ps} motion; shee will be content to release all her charges, also the moyety of tharrerages aforesaide although with exceeding clamor he hath justly moved her to afford him no favour.'[1]

The difficulty of the case, which the Court of Exchequer and the Lord Treasurer himself seemed unable to resolve, was that the sequestered lands were originally Mrs Shelley's property, not her husband's, and that they ought to revert to her on his death. Byrd, who was not a rich man, felt that after all that he had paid both by way of purchase money (e.g. the £300 paid to Hollingworth) and by way of improvement of the estate, he had some rights to the enjoyment of the

---

[1] *Exchequer Decrees and Orders*, 7 Jas. I.

14

estate. He is said to have ' altered some barne
doors, erected chimneys, made partitions, and
at a cost of £150 to have brought water into the
house in pipes of lead '. On the other hand it
must have seemed very unfair to Mrs Shelley that
lands sequestered as part of a religious persecution
should be handed over to one who, also a Catholic,
suffered no more than petty vexations for his
religion. Byrd certainly seems to have asserted
what he deemed to be his rights against her if
not with animosity at any rate with vigour. Her
fourth complaint makes it appear that the last
part of the King's letter had rankled with her.
The modesty of her final demand seems to indicate
that the financial claims which she made against
Byrd were really an attempt to damage Byrd's
reputation for honesty as a retaliation for the
defamation of character which she felt she had
suffered at his hands. The long-drawn suit was
not finally settled till, on the death of Mrs Shelley
in 1610, Byrd purchased the estate outright from
her son.

Besides his investments in land, we know of
another financial operation in which Byrd was
concerned. This, however, belongs to the early
part of his career and connects him, quite
innocently, with one of the notorious abuses of
of the age—the monopolies granted to individuals
by the Crown.

On January 22nd, 1575, a licence was granted
jointly to Tallis and Byrd giving them the

monopoly of printing and selling music and music paper. By this the Queen

> 'graunted full priviledge and licence unto our wel-beloved servaunts Thomas Tallis and William Birde Gentl. of our Chapell, and to the overlyver of them, & to the assignees of them and of the surviver of them, for xxi. yeares next ensuing, to imprint any and so many as they will of set songe or songes in partes, either in English, Latine, French, Italian or other tongues that may serve for musicke either in Churche or chamber, or otherwise to be either plaid or soonge, And that that they may rule and cause to be ruled by impression any paper to serve for printing or pricking of any songe or songes, and may sell and utter any printed bokes or papers of any songe or songes, or any bookes or quieres of such ruled paper imprinted.'

It was also forbidden

> 'to bring or cause to be brought out of any forren Realmes into any our dominions any songe or songes made and printed in any forren countrie, to sell or put to sale, uppon paine of our high displeasure.'

As a mark of gratitude the two composers dedicated their joint work the *Cantiones Sacrae*[1] of 1575 to the Queen. But the privilege was a source of loss not gain to them, so that two years later they petitioned for an annuity. The petition says that ' Bird and Tallys, her maiesties

---

[1] This book was printed by Thomas Vautrollier. The title page bears the formula Cum Privilegio, but there is no mention as in later publication of the printer having an assignation from the patentees. The patent was granted as early in the year as Jan. 22, and the book must have been issued *after* the grant, for the licence is printed at the end of the part books.

servauntes, . . . haue musike bokes with
note, which the complainantes confesse they
wold not print nor be furnished to print though
there were no priuilege.' The petitioners
therefore sought a less ambiguous privilege
and asked for the revenue of a lease. Tallis
'having served the Queen with her ancestors
about forty years' made the request on the
ground of his age, Byrd on the ground that
he was underpaid—though it was naturally
not presented to the royal ears in terms so bald.
The petition states that Byrd 'being called to
Her Majesty's service from Lincoln Cathedral,
when he was well settled, is now through great
charge of wife and children, fallen into debt and
great necessity. By reason of his daily attendance
in the Queen's service he is letted from reaping
such commodity by teaching as heretofore he
did. Her grant two years ago of a licence for
printing music has fallen out to their loss and
hindrance to the value of 200 marks at least.'

The annuity was granted, but the monopoly
still remained in their hands and after Tallis's
death in 1585 became Byrd's sole property. He
must have made some arrangement with Thomas
East, who appears as his assignee on the title page
of the 1588 set of madrigals ' which are to be sold
at the dwelling house of the said T. East, by
Paules Wharfe '. East continued to print after
Byrd's interest in the business had expired at the
end of the twenty-one years (i.e. in 1596). Two

years later Byrd's pupil Morley obtained a similar licence, which does not appear to have been extinguished by the bill for the Abolition of Monopolies which Parliament thrust upon a reluctant queen in 1601, since references to the licence are found on title pages of a much later date. From the petition of Tallis and Byrd it appears that Byrd was a poor man at the beginning of his career, and his early poverty may account for the zeal with which he strove to retain the property of Stondon and for the careful finance which Mrs Shelley declared he practised at her expense. His career was certainly one which we should nowadays describe as successful, for there is plenty of evidence to show that he stood well with various influential patrons. Among it is a curious letter from the Earl of Northumberland to Lord Burghley dated February 28th, 1579, and endorsed ' Bird of ye Chappell ' :

> ' My dere good lorde I amme ernestly required to be a suiter to your l(ordship) for this berer, M^r berde, that your l wyll have hime in remẽbrance w̃h your fauer towardes hime seinge he cane not inioye that wyche was his first sutte (suit) and granted unto hime. I ame the more importenat to your l for that he is my frend and cheffly that he is scolle-master to my daughter in his artte. The mane is honeste and one whom I knowe your l may comande.'

It is not known what was the nature of this suit, but the letter is one more testimony to the universal respect in which Byrd seems to have been held by all his contemporaries except those with whom he engaged in legal disputes. The Earl of Worcester, to whom the 1588 volume of madrigals was dedicated, seems to have employed Byrd as his private musician, for Byrd's will reveals the fact that he had rooms in the Earl's town house ' It(em) I give & bequeth unto my sonne Thomas Byrd all my goods in my lodginge In the Earle of wosters house in the straund.' Worcester, in Queen Elizabeth's opinion, reconciled ' what she believed impossible a stiff papist and a good subject ', and it is more than likely that much of the Latin church music which Byrd wrote was composed for private celebrations of the Mass in his private chapel. It is significant that Byrd dedicated the first volume of *Cantiones Sacrae* (1589) to Worcester. In the dedicatory address he writes that in all the distinguished company of the nobility (in tota hac nobilium nostrorũ celeberrima corona) no one showed more know-ledge or love of music (Musicae peritiorem aut . . . amantiorem), and speaks further of his wonted kindness and affection (solita in me humanitate ac amore) towards one who was included in the Earl's circle of patronage (in tuis clientelis numerato). It was the Earl of Worcester, too, who made the remark about Byrd's *Lullaby* in a letter to the Earl of Shrewsbury[1] The Earl of Northampton also seems to have

[1] See above, p. 171.

helped Byrd in some of his personal difficulties, i.e., presumably his encounters with the law as a recusant or in his suits over his property. Byrd dedicated the first volume of the *Gradualia* to him and in it says ' You were, and if I am not mistaken still are, a most kind patron to me in my family's troubles' (Te habui, atque etiam, ni fallor, habeo, in afflictis familiæ meæ rebus benignissmum patronum) and he also refers to an increase in the salaries of the Gentlemen of the Chapel which were obtained by the Earl's efforts in 1604. Other dedications to Sir Christopher Hatton, Lord Lumley, Lord Hunsdon, Lord Petre, and Lord Cumberland are evidence not only of the interest of the aristocracy in music, but also the high respect in which Byrd was held. It was of course customary for musicians to seek these influential patrons, but the actual terms of Byrd's dedications seem to reflect something more than a mere convention. Aristocratic patronage and the royal favour undoubtedly preserved Byrd, as they had done several musicians before him, from religious persecution. There is the parallel case of Sebastian Westcote, organist and master of the children at St Paul's, who is described by a contemporary (in 1561) as ' ita charus Elizabethæ fuit ut nihil schismaticæ agens, locum suum in ea ecclesia retineat ' (he has been such a favourite of Elizabeth that since he does not carry his schism into action he keeps his place in that church). It seems possible, however, that nothing sufficed to save him altogether from the unpleasant consequences of being a recusant during the 'period of silence' from 1591 to 1605, during which he published nothing. 'In afflictis familiæ meæ' may refer to a time when he had to make himself as inconspicuous as possible.

Mr Barclay Squire, who has discovered most of what we know about Byrd's personal history, has recently found a reference to the composer in the annals of Cambridge. As already recorded[1] he wrote a three-part song *Preces Deo fundamus* for a performance of Thomas Legge's Latin play *Ricardus III* at St John's College. But another Cambridge connection in which he is alleged to have been a 'wayght of the said University' is quite incredible, and the whole episode in which his name is put forward as a candidate for the office of Lord of the Tappes is incomprehensible. On September 7th, 1583, the vice-chancellor professed to appoint Byrde to this undignified office by the following high-sounding document[2]:

John Bell D.D. Vice-Chancellor of the University of Cambridge, to all and singular the Queens Mayestys loving Subjects, repairing unto the fair called Sturbridge fair, sendeth greeting in our Lord everlasting. Whereas time out of minde, it hath been a custome and always used within this fair, that some musitian, whome they have usually called the Lord of the Tappes, should

---

[1] p. 191, supra.
[2] C. H. Cooper, *Annals of Cambridge*, Vol. V, p. 914.

for the safety of the Booths & profit of the Marchants after sun set & likewise before the sunne rising by sounde of some Instrument, give notice to shut & open the shops. And that of late one John Pattyn, which for many years had that roome, is now departed this world. In consideration whereof, many of the worshipfull Citizens of London & other places have desired one other to be placed in that roome, & for that cause hath commended unto us William Byrde the bearer hereof, being a Musitian and now servant & wayght of the said University. We the said Vice-chancellor, willing to pleasure the said worshipfull citizens & other occupiers, have given and granted, & by these presents do give & grant unto the said W. Byrde the said roome and place of the Lord of Tappes, to continue therein during our pleasure, upon his good usage and honest behaviour. In witness whereof we the said Vicechancellor have to these presents set the seal of our office. Given at Cambridge, the 7th day of Sept., in the 25th year of the Reign of our Sovereign Lady Eliz., &c. an. 1583.'

MS. Baker iii. 428.

There are several difficulties about this. Sturbridge Fair was one of the battlegrounds and one of the *casus belli* of the town and gown rows of the sixteenth century. Each side claimed certain rights in the fair, each side had a pecuniary interest in it, each side appointed a 'watch' to patrol it and to protect those rights and interests. Collisions as might be expected were not infrequent and about this time feeling ran high. Dr Bell's arrogation to himself of the right of appointing a

217

watchman 'for the safety of the Booths and profit of the Marchants' may therefore have been a move in the dispute for control of the fair and the revenues it brought in, or it may have been intended to annoy the Protestants of Cambridge by choosing a Romanist for what was perhaps a sinecure. Whatever the explanation of this curious document, it is impossible to believe that a Gentleman of the Chapel could have been seriously appointed to an office of which the duties were those of a glorified bell-man or that the dignified Byrd could ever have played the clown as Lord of the Tappes. For unless he had completely changed his character in a hundred years he was a frivolous dignitary, 'an old fellow arm'd all over with spiggots and fossets, like a porcupine with his quills, or looking rather like a fowl wrapped up in a pound of sausages', as a writer of 1700 described him. We can only conclude on present evidence either that this Byrd was not our Byrd, or that the office was a non-resident sinecure like other University offices of later times, such as the rectorships of Scottish universities which are filled nowadays in the same irrelevant manner after an electoral contest on political issues.

Byrd had five, if not six, children. Four only are mentioned in his will. His eldest son, Christopher, seems to have estranged him during his later years, and a fourth daughter may have been the Anne Byrd who is mentioned in the proceedings against the Shelley family and may have predeceased him. His second son was Thomas, his daughters were Elizabeth, Rachel and Mary, all of whom were twice married. His will shows that he was a precise person and that with the exception of his eldest son, whom he disinherits, he disposed of his property to his children and their heirs in strict accordance with their seniority while imposing, as was just, obligations on those who received the estates to pay allowances to their juniors. His daughter-in-law, Catherine, who had taken his side against her husband in the differences, whatever they were, that caused the estrangement, was to inherit Stondon and to be one of his executors.

> 'And wheire I have beene longe desireous to setle my poore estate in the ffearme of Stondon place accordinge to an awarde latlye made betweene Catheren Byrde my daughter in law & mee bee a very good ffrend to hus both:[1] wch award wee both give our cristian pmisses to peforme: but havinge beene letted and hyndred theirein : by the undutifull obstinancie of one whome I am unwilling to name : doe nowe ordayne & disposse of the same as ffolloweth : ffirst the whole ffearme to remayne to my selfe & my assignes duringe my lyfe : and after my desscease : I give the same to my daughter in law m^{ris} Catheren Byrd for her life : upon the condicoñs folowinge'

and here follow a number of claims upon the estates for rent of adjoining farms and annuities

---

[1] 'Hus' presumably means Byrd and his wife, who was dead by now.

for Thomas and Rachel. The one whom he is unwilling to name must be his son Christopher, to whose son Thomas, however, the succession is to go. To his own son Thomas he bequeathed all the goods in his London lodgings in the Earl of Worcester's house.[1] But he seems to have been apprehensive of the goodwill of this son also, or else he may have had evidence that Thomas had inherited his father's passion for litigation, for he makes express provision for the disposal of a certain annuity which he bequeathes to his daughter Elizabeth :

> ' I doe now declare how it shall bee dispossed of after my sayde daughters desscease first yf my sayde sonne Thomas Byrde concurr wth this my last will & Testament & except of his Annyty accordinge to ye same : . . . Allwayes pvided yt yf my sonne Thomas Byrd to seeke by lawe or other wayes to disturb or troble my executors (his sister-in-law and his nephew and name-sake, Catherine's son, Thomas) & not agree to ye same : Then I doe heireby declare That my will and intention is : That the sayde Thomas Byrde my sonne shall have noe parte of the sayde Annyty : but I doe heireby give y^t part of ye annyty That I had given to my sonne Thomas Byrd : to Thomas Byrd my granchild to hym and his heires for ever.'

They were not an easygoing lot, these Byrds, and when they disagreed they stuck to their points of view with the greatest obstinacy. Obviously the old man feared that the middle-aged man

[1] See above, p. 214.

would be jealous of the young man; it may well be that Thomas Byrd senior sympathized with his elder brother for the treatment the latter had received from the unholy alliance of father, wife and son—three against one. Byrd made this will on November 15th, 1622; rather less than eight months later he died. His death is recorded in the Cheque Book of the Chapel Royal: ' 1623. William Byrd, a Father of Musick, died the fourth of July, and John Croker a counter-tenor of Westminster was admitted . . . for a yeare of probacion.' It is most likely that he was buried, as he requested in his will, in the churchyard at Stondon, but the parish registers of this period have not survived, and it is not known with certainty where his last resting place is. Catherine Byrd continued to live at Stondon, but did not carry out her obligations under the will, as the Court of Chancery on October 10th, 1635, made an order to pay the annuities due to Thomas and Rachel which she had not attempted to do since Byrd's death. A year or two later the house was occupied by a John Leigh and in 1651 by one of the Petre family, who also seems not to have discharged his obligations, for the Committee for Compounding with Delinquents was approached on behalf of Thomas Byrd who was dependent on the annuity of £20 which had not been paid. Thomas's original annuity under his father's will was £10, but by this time he had apparently increased his holding in the property and it was represented to the Committee that he 'is seventy-five years old and has no other means of subsistence'. The Petre family had had their goods seized for recusancy and their refusal to pay this rent seems almost like a repetition of Byrd's struggles with Mrs Shelley. In any case the complicated tenure of the property led to a great deal of quarrelling and litigation, as one after another those in possession are found refusing point blank to pay demands from other claimants. The property soon after this was sold and passed out of the possession of the Byrd family. In 1877 Stondon Place was burned down, so that the present building has no associations with the composer.

We hear of a brother of the composer in a State Paper[1] quoted in *Troubles of our Catholic Forefathers*.[2] When Benjamin Tichborne was let out of prison on the condition that he would act as a spy on his fellow Catholics, his first letter to Lord Keeper Puckering dated May 28th, 1594, reported 'meeting with one Byrd, brother to Byrd of the Chapel. I understand that Mrs Tregian, Mrs Charnock & Mrs Sybil Tregian will be here at the Court (i.e. Greenwich) to-day.' The name Tregian is interesting in this connection (Cf. above, p. 132).

In forming an estimate of Byrd as a musician we may very well take as a starting point the

[1] Public Record Office, *Dom. Eliz.*, ccxlviii, n. 118.
[2] Vol. II, p. 143.

opinions of him held by his contemporaries, who seem one and all to have regarded him with the very highest esteem. Morley and Tomkins, both excellent composers of madrigals, were pupils of Byrd and may therefore be suspected of a biassed enthusiasm, yet they both testify to a tremendous respect not untinged with awe, similar to that in which Beethoven was held by his friends, for one who towered above ordinary men. Morley dedicated to Byrd his *Plaine and Easie Intro-duction to Practicall Musicke* in order ' to notifie vnto your selfe in some sort the entire loue and unfained affection which I beare unto you.' He seeks for his work such a patron ' as both with iudgement may correct it, and with authority defend him from the rash censures of such as thinke they gaine great praise in condemning others.' In the course of the work he says of Byrd that he is ' never without reverence to be named of the musicians ', and Tomkins, who in other dedications says quite shortly ' To Dr Dowland ' or ' To Master John Coprario ' and at the most ' To my deare Father Mr Thomas Tomkins ', becomes almost loquacious in the dedication of No. 14 of his *Songs* ' To my ancient and much reverenced Master, William Byrd '. Henry Peacham[1] reflects the same feeling on the part of the cultured classes. He writes immediately after the sentence about reading at sight which has already been quoted[2] :

[1] *The Compleat Gentleman,* 1622.   [2] Supra, p. 152.

'To deliver you my opinion, whom among other Authors you should imitate and allow for the best, there being so many equally good, is somewhat difficult ; yet as in the rest herein you shall have my opinion.

'For Motets and Musick of piety and devotion, as well for the honour of our Nation, as the merit of the man, I prefer above all our *Phœnix* M. William Byrd, whom in that kind, I know not whether any may equall, I am sure none excell, even by the judgment of France and Italy, who are very sparing in the commendation of strangers, in regard of that conceipt they hold of themselves. His *Cantiones Sacræ*, as also his *Gradualia* are meer Angelicall and Divine ; and being of himself naturally disposed to Gravity and Piety, his vein is not so much for leight Madrigals or Canzonets ; yet his Virginellæ and some others in his first Set, cannot be mended by the best Italian of them all.'

This is illuminating in more ways than one, though the remark about his vein not being so much for light madrigals has been taken out of its context and has given a distorted idea of the quality of his madrigals. Note 'the merit of the man' which seems to imply a respect for the composer's character which was esteemed in a way that was not altogether possible to Beethoven's admirers. Note the traditional attitude of continental countries to English music, unwarrantable at this period if excusable in the nineteenth century. Byrd's reputation, however, seems to have gone abroad without his having himself widely travelled like Dowland. *Phœnix* may refer to his senile vigour, but it might more appropriately signify the new birth which came over English music as a result of Byrd's work. Another estimate of a man whose opinion is worth having is that of John Baldwin. This man was a chorister of St George's Chapel, Windsor, a great copyist of music and a modest composer. His knowledge of music therefore was very wide. In a versified conspectus of the music in common use at the time which he appended to a MS. collection of motets and instrumental pieces[1] he mentions the names of the chief of the earlier English composer then of various Italian masters :

Luca Merensio with others manie moe,
As Philipp Demonte the Emperours man also ;
And Orlando by name and eeke Crequillion,
Cipriano Rore : and also Andreon.
All famous in there arte, there is of that no doute :
There workes no lesse declare in everie place aboute,
Yet let not straingers bragg, nor they these soe
commende,
For they may now geve place and sett themselves
behynde,
An Englishman, by name, William Birde for his skill.
Which I should heve sett first, for soe it was my
will,
Whose greater skill & knowledge dothe excelle all at
this tyme

[1] Royal Library, now on loan to Brit. Mus., reprinted by Miss Andrewes in her edition of *My Lady Nevell's Booke*.

And far to strange countries abroade his skill dothe
    shyne;
Famous men be abroad and skilful in the arte
I do confesse the same and not from it starte;
But in Ewroppe is none like to our Englishe man,
Which dothe so farre exceede as trulie I it scan.
As ye cannot finde out his equale in all thinges
Throwghe out the worlde so wide, and so his fame now
    ringes.
With fingers and with penne he hathe not now his peere;
For in this worlde so wide is none can him come neere;
The rarest man he is in musicks worthy arte
That now on earthe doth liue: I speake it from my
    harte
Or heere to fore hath been or after him shall come
None suche I feare shall rise that may be calde his
    sonne.

The same scribe transcribed in his beautiful
hand the collection of virginal pieces for Lady
Nevell, and at the end of one of them he cannot
restrain his enthusiasm and writes, mr. w. Birde,
homo memorabilis.[1] There are several other
instances of the irresistible impulse to marginal
commentary which Byrd's music evoked in his
admirers. In a MS. set of part books in Christ
Church library belonging to the years 1581-5 the
copyist, smarting under the reproach which was
levelled against these islands in B.C. 50 as in
A.D. 1900 of being a land without music, quotes an
offending passage from Cicero's letters:[2] Britannici
belli exitus expectatur: etiam illud jam cognitum

---

[1] Not *mirabilis*.   [2] Cicero, *ad Atticum*, lib. 4.

est, neque argenti scrupulum esse ullum in ea insula, neque ullam spem prædæ, nisi ex mancipiis, ex quibus nullos puto te literis aut musica eruditos expectare. (The end of the British war is awaited : this much at any rate is certain already that there is not a grain of silver in the island, nor is there any hope of spoils, unless it be slaves, and none of these I suspect will you find practised in literature or music.) To which the triumphant rejoinder is added : Unus Birdus omnes Anglos ab hoc convicio prorsus liberat (One Bird frees all Englishmen from this charge henceforward). *Prorsus* apparently did not include the nineteenth century ! There are several other notes in the same manuscript :

Birde, suos jactet si Musa Britanna clientes
　　Signiferium turmis te creet illa suis.
(If Bird, the Muse of Britain parades her retainers 'tis you whom she will make standard-bearer of her companies).

Cantores inter, quod in æthere sol, bone Birde ;
Cur arctant laudes disticha nostra tuas.
　　(Thou art among singers, good Bird, as the sun is in the heavens ; why do our couplets fall short of your renown ?)

In the tenor book, after No. 37 :

Ut lucem solis sequitur lux proxima luna
Sic tu post Birdum Munda secunde venis.
(As the moon follows next to the sun's light
So you, Munday, come second after Bird).

The comentator however, is equally enthusiastic about White, Parsons and Tallis, though he does not mention them so frequently, and he often adds comments in praise of music itself.

The title 'Father of Music' was more than once bestowed on Byrd by his contemporaries. It appears first in the 1575 volume of *Cantiones Sacræ* in which Byrd is placed on the same level as Tallis. There is an anonymous poem, *De Anglorum Musica* in which the wisdom of dedicating the work to the Queen is commended.

> Ergo patronatu tam doctæ Principis aucta
> Oras nullius gentis, et ora timet
> Tallisium Birdumque suos testata parentes
> Audacter quo non ore canenda venit.

[N.B. Musica is the subject of the sentence.]

(And so Music, reinforced by the patronage of so learned a Princess, fears no country's talk nor territory. But having sworn allegiance to Tallis and Byrd as its parents, boldly comes to every lip for singing.)

Similarly in the second book of *Gradualia* a someone who calls himself G. Ga. writes a far-fetched epigram about the difference between ancient augury and modern music and he inscribes it to

> Amicissimo mihi, multis colendo
> omnibus suspiciendo, D. Guliemo Byrde
> Britanniae Musicae Parenti.

(To one who is a very dear friend to me, is courted by many and admired by all, William Byrd, the father of British music.)

' A Father of Musicke ' was also written against
his name in the Chapel Royal Cheque Book by
the clerk who recorded his death. These three
allusions seem to indicate the recognition by his
contemporaries that he was a pioneer of English
music, and the tone of the introductory poems
points in the same direction. Baldwin's survey
of the world's music and the high place taken in it
by Byrd has already been mentioned, but the
Latin poems of Mulcaster and Richardson which
were prefixed to the 1575 *Cantiones Sacræ*
explicitly speak of the British Muse choosing
Tallis and Byrd to make her fame known abroad
at a time when the great Queen's glory seemed
to demand that Britain should not be silent
and leave the composing of music entirely to
Italians.

Richardson's actual reference to the two
composers is

> Tallisius magno dignus honore senex
> Et Birdus tantum natus decorare magistrum.

(Tallis grown old and worthy to be held in great
honour and Bird born to be an ornament to such a
teacher.)

One other contemporary testimony to Byrd has
already been quoted. Nicholas Yonge in the
introduction to *Musica Transalpina* explaining
why he is providing songs with an English text
says : ' And albeit there be some English songs
lately set forth by a great Maister of Musicke,

which for skill and sweetness may content the most curious.' And he adds ' yet because they are not many in number, men delighted with varietie, have wished more of the same sort ', which shows how the demand for madrigals became suddenly large after 1588.

His contemporaries therefore seem to have entertained no doubt as to his greatness as a composer. A more remarkable comment is found in a part-book of anthems belonging to Ely Cathedral where, in handwriting of the eighteenth century when admiration of the Elizabethan masters was not fashionable, someone has put against the name of Byrd the words ' ye inimitable '.

And how are we to estimate him after three centuries of neglect ? We are debarred by this very neglect from making a final valuation, for there is no one sufficiently acquainted with all his works to compare them with the corresponding works of other composers in other countries. His Latin Church music may be compared with Palestrina's, and though he is a bold man who would pull down Palestrina from his unique pinnacle and set Byrd in his place, the mere fact that Byrd may be compared with him without impropriety puts the English composer at once among the great ones of music. He was also like Palestrina in being a prolific composer, but unlike him in being versatile, in which respect he may justly be compared with Bach. His instrumental work is necessarily more tentative than the latter's, if only from the fact that he was born 150 years earlier. As a madrigalist in spite of some very notable exceptions, he is not perhaps the equal either of the great Italians, Orlando di Lassus and the rest, or of his own great followers, Morley, Weelkes and Wilbye. But if we estimate at its full value his pioneer work, such as that for the English church service and the developments he made in instrumental style, and add that to the sheer musical value of his best compositions, we are bound to admit him to the small band of first-rank composers and to allow him to dispute with Purcell the title of the foremost British composer.

To be a pioneer in music means something rather different from being a pioneer in anything else, because the progress of the art is inevitably a more gradual process than breaking into new country for the first time. Yet even in so concrete a field as the exploration of the surface of the globe those who, like Columbus and The Ancient Mariner can say

> We were the first that ever burst
> Into that silent sea,

owe the idea that lies behind their attempt to some other pioneer who was fired with the notion of sailing some other uncharted ocean, and they may come after many another Ulysses who has been driven to turn back or has been washed down into the gulf. He who scales Everest will be less of a pioneer than those who have made the first attempts. In music every pioneer always seems to have a predecessor ; no one ever seems to have done anything for the first time. Music advances along one broad highway, and every composer who would reach new country must reach it along that road. Wagner, the great revolutionary of opera, looks back to Gluck, Gluck to Monteverde, Monteverde to the experimenters who gathered in Bardi's palace in Florence, they to the mystery plays and to Greek tragedy. The sonatas of Beethoven derive from Haydn, Haydn from C. P. E. Bach, he from his greater father, and Bach himself did not invent the form of his suites. The modern orchestra goes back to broken consorts, and they in turn to the instrumental accompaniments of the vocal music of the Middle Ages and ultimately to Greece and Egypt. The songs of Schubert are of the same family as the lutenist's ayres, which are descended from the songs of the troubadors and so go straight to primitive folk-song. The pioneers are those who, finding something of value, enrich it so that it almost becomes something else. Byrd was not the first to write virginal music or music for the English liturgy, but he is the first who counts. His song, *My Little Sweet Darling*, is only one out of many pieces of incidental music to the choir-boy plays of the period, but it is also the first song in the modern sense. Many Italians and a few

Englishmen had written madrigals before him, but he is the first English composer to take up this form of composition in a big way, and he is the founder of a school. Music had been played on viols before Byrd was born, yet he was the first Englishman to write a work for strings alone which can rank with the string quartets of later times. There is no need to recapitulate all the innovations which stand to his credit in the music which has been examined in detail in previous chapters. It is plain that in spite of the conservatism of his temperament he is by far the greatest musical pioneer who has ever lived in this country, and in the whole range of music he can only be compared with Monteverde, who resembled him in maintaining alongside of his innovations the power to write also in an older style. What he did for the keyboard can only be compared with the modifications of instrumental style effected by Chopin. Byrd's English church music corresponds in a way with Bach's church cantatas; but Bach was no pioneer, and the amazing fertility of his invention is balanced by Byrd's success in creating a new means of expression to meet a new need. For his harmonic venturesomeness he himself feels that some apology is needed, but with characteristic firmness he withdraws nothing. 'In the expressing of these songs', he says in the Epistle to the Reader in his 1588 set of madrigals, ' either by voyces or Instruments, if ther happen to be any jarre or

233

dissonãce,[1] blame not the Printer, who (I doe assure thee) through his great paines and diligence doth heere deliver to thee a perfect and true Coppie.' Is there then in the whole history of music, which has a close-wrought unity like a living organism, any composer who made so many innovations, anyone who has half the claim to the title pioneer and at the same time to the prouder title of great composer ?

What kind of man was this conservative radical ? We have little more than the music to tell us, and to attempt a psychological portrait with such material is a hazardous business. With the facts of his biography, however, and the testimonies of his contemporaries to restrain us, we may hope to produce a picture of the composer in which the features are definite yet not improbable, the character something more than an insubstantial shade yet less highly speculative than that of another William contemporary with him. The first thing to note is that as in most musical genuises his ability manifests itself young—he was a cathedral organist at twenty and at the top of the tree as a composer at thirty-two. If the madrigal[2] *Crowned with flowers and lillies*, which is an elegy on the death of Queen Mary, was written at the time of her death, when Byrd would be

[1] Allusions have been made to the peculiarities of Byrd's style as occasion has prompted in going through his music. For a general discussion the reader may be referred to Canon Fellowes's *English Madrigal Composers* and to Dr. Ernest Walker's *History of Music in England*.

[2] Mr Barclay Squire assigns it to the reign of James I.

fifteen, it does something towards conferring on him the status of prodigy and allows him to associate with the young Brahms and the youthful Wagner, though not quite with the infant Mozart. That he was not above the intellectual excitements of musical chess and could exult in his powers is shown by his canonic motet *Diliges Dominum*. Another quality not so much of mind as of temperament appears early from his close association with Tallis. The prefaces he wrote to his various publications betray a certain modesty, which must have sweetened his relations with the elder man. It is certainly a pleasing spectacle to contemplate—even from this distance of time—the apparent absence of jealousy and presence of mutual esteem and affection between these two artists (master and disciple), joint organists, colleagues in business,[1] and fellow composers. Such associations are not too common in the history of music, though the abdication of Blow from the Westminster organ in favour of his pupil, Henry Purcell, if we believe the tradition, always encourages our faith in the magnanimity of musicians. The close association of Tallis and Byrd is a credit to them both, and it drew even from Burney a shrewd estimate of Byrd's character. ' Of Byrd's moral character and natural disposition there can perhaps be no testimony more favourable or less subject to suspicion, than those of rival professors, with whom he appears to have lived,

[1] See above, p. 201, for the monopoly of music printing which they enjoyed.

during a long life, with cordiality and friendship. And of the goodness of his heart it is to me no trivial proof, that he loved and was beloved by his master Tallis, and scholar, Morley; who from their intimate connexion with him, must have seen him *en robe de chambre*, and been spectators of all the operations of temper, in the opposite situations of subjection and dominion.'

The great German musicians were mostly men of little cultivation outside their music, but Byrd seems to have been both intelligent and well educated. He could hardly have pursued his various objectives through the law-courts unless he had been a man with an acute mind. According to Anthony Wood he was "excellent in mathematics." His English prefaces show sound sense and a feeling for style. He wrote excellent Latin, as the prefaces to his volumes of *Cantiones Sacræ* and *Gradualia* testify. He was a literary musician and definitely belongs to the class of composers, mostly to be found in the nineteenth century, who are definitely susceptible to words. He has given expression to the effect they had on him in one of those bursts of confidence which composers are rarely able to make about their own mental processes when they are engaged in the act of composition. In the preface to the first book of *Gradualia* he writes to his patron that he had been moved to emulate the swan, which sings more sweetly on the approach of death, by two considerations: ' duo habui non mediocria sive præsidia sive incitamenta. Alterum fuit; verborum ipsorum dulcitudo : alterum dignitas tua ' (I had two far from negligible excuses, not to say inducements : the one was the appeal of the words themselves, the other the esteem in which you are held). And he proceeds to elaborate the view that the sacredness of the subject demands the best work of which he is capable. Then he adds : ' Porro, illis ipsis sententiis (ut experiendo didici) adeo abstrusa atque recondita vis inest ; ut divina cogitanti diligenterque ac serio pervolutanti ; nescio quonam modo, aptissimi quique numeri, quasi sponte accurrant sua ; animoque minime ignavo atque inerti liberaliter ipsi sese offerant.' (Furthermore, there is in those very sentiments— as I have learned by experience—a mysterious hidden power, so that to anyone who considers carefully the divine mysteries and seriously ponders them in his heart the most appropriate strains occur of their own accord in some strange way and offer themselves copiously even when one's mind is sluggish and inactive). He speaks elsewhere of his music being ' framed to the life of the words ' and we have seen in the music itself that this is a just claim. And not in any narrow sense, either, for the Alleluias of his Latin motets and the Amens of his English anthems seem to contain the spirit of the preceding words crystallized as it were in an epilogue.

His long life and enormous output show that he was a person of great vitality, yet he seems to have been without the physical gusto of living which characterized his great contemporaries on so many fields of human activity. The outstanding feature of his temperament seems to have been his gravity, which gives the key to his whole character. If we would know what manner of man he was, we have only to look at a not uncommon type of Quaker, not perhaps the 'Young Friend' nor the somewhat narrow type of old-fashioned Friend, but the enlightened Quaker who grew up in the last quarter of the nineteenth century. We see in him the same grave demeanour, the same fundamental seriousness, the same firmness in matters of conscience (e.g. his unswerving devotion to the Catholic faith). 'Being of himself naturally disposed to Gravity and Piety' says Peacham, and the other contemporary references to him imply a profound respect similar to that which is accorded to Quakers by all kinds of people who have nothing in common with their outlook. But of this quality the music itself, especially the sacred music, is the best testimony, with its mingled depth, austerity and sweetness. The 'Earl of Salisbury' pavan might almost be a portrait in music of its composer. So might the little grace *Deo Gratias* in *Gradualia I*. That there was a human heart beating behind this grave exterior is shown by the graciousness of the lullabies, the winsomeness of the virginal variations on popular tunes, the shy and rare but quite real sense of

fun by madrigals like *Though Amaryllis dance
in green.* When men of serious mind and grave
manner unbend, the relaxation lends additional
charm to their smiles.

That William Byrd was a Quaker fifty years
before George Fox was born is shown by a number
of qualities, some fundamental, some more
superficial, which he shares with ' birthright '
Friends who have been brought up in the Quaker
way of life. Friends are unfortunately not
musical; generations of artistic repression have
done much to crush out the aptitude for music
which the more enlightened attitude now
prevalent in the Society cannot immediately
repair. But if this accident of circumstance is
overlooked, it will be apparent that Byrd had a
religious mind of a temper like that of the
Quakers. The conscious but unobtrusive reference of all things in life to its religious purpose may
be seen in the opening sentence of his will[1] and in
the eighth reason to persuade everyone to learn
to sing.[2] There is a recognized similarity between
Roman Catholicism and Quakerism in that each
is a mystical religion, i.e. each bases its faith on an
immediate experience and comprehension of
divine mysteries, the Quaker in the Inner Light,
the Roman Catholic in the Mass and in retreats
for contemplation. That Byrd's mind was of
this kind is revealed everywhere in the Latin
church music, or—to quote a specific instance—in

[1] See p. 194.   [2] See p. 159.

the well-known *Ave Verum Corpus*. He was not content, as most Roman Catholics are, to accept from authority a ready-made view of religious truths; 'divina cogitanti diligenterque ac serio pervolutanti' are his own words, and the music which he fashioned for the sentences on which he pondered show his individual thought. In this context the English Church music provides corroborative evidence, for it is 'framed to the life of the words' no less than the Latin even if it has not always the same emotional glow. His complete absence of bigotry combined with his tenacious adherence to his own faith shows a balance of qualities rarely achieved. The Great Service, to look no further, shows that having accepted the necessity of writing for the reformed church he did it not perfunctorily nor irreverently nor even with any want of sympathy, but with all the powers that he could command, while his prosecutions for recusancy show his unswerving fidelity to what in his own heart he felt to be the truth for him. This tenacity he showed too in the ordinary affairs of life, as his frequent lawsuits prove: 'The mane is honeste', says the Earl of Northumberland; and though we ought not to attach a too literally modern meaning to the word 'honest', we feel in surveying his life that he had that integrity of character which allowed him to amass a modest property without forfeiting the respect of his fellows in much the same way as Friends have throughout the history of their Society successfully conducted their businesses. His tidy mind and sense of strict justice appear in his will; the vigour and enterprise of his mind are shown in the spirit he displays in his music where he is bold in pioneering yet never reckless. Like many Friends he appears to have had a sharp tongue. 'Vile and bitter words', says Mrs Shelley, but she was prejudiced. We may, however, be sure that he did not mince his words; and though there is no bitterness in the reference in his will to the son of whom he disapproved there is no concealment of his strong disapprobation. His industriousness is shown by his vast output of work, and his conscientiousness appears not only in the fact that he discharged his duties at the Chapel Royal assiduously, but in the tone of his addresses to the reader in his published works, in which he expresses his solicitude for the advancement of the art of music.

Those who are familiar with the Society of Friends will recognize the similarity of Byrd's whole personality to the kind of personality which is typical of a body which is still a somewhat close corporation, whose members for all their strong individuality still bear marked characteristics peculiar to their Society and its outlook on life. The similarity is extraordinarily striking, and the only two qualities which differentiate him from the typical Quaker beside the fact that he was a musician are his absence of humour and his feeling for romance. There are touches of humour as we have seen in one or two of the madrigals, but it is rare ; and in the gay Elizabethan age which produced Shakespeare and in music Thomas Morley, Byrd would appear as lacking in humour. His continual references in the works published after 1611 to swan songs, ' ultimum vale-s ', ' last travailes in this sort ' from a man who lived another fifteen years or so and showed himself throughout his life as a person of exceptional vitality indicates a lack of proportion in his outlook which a sense of humour would ·have corrected. There are distinct traces of a feeling for romance in the virginal music though not much elsewhere, and as we gather that he was a brilliant performer we may be fairly sure that his gravity was enlivened with a touch of fancy which seems to reside in the sprightly instrument itself and which must have informed the performances of the writer of *The Carman's Whistle*.

In William Byrd the forces that made England a " nest of singing birds " found their first and most powerful expression. He was the father of the madrigalists and of the virginal composers. The present revival of English music is being fertilized by a renewal of interest in this very Tudor Music. Byrd exercised an enormous influence in his day, which ceased and seemed to be quite lost when the great Germans came on the scene. But now it is beginning to be felt again as we turn once more after centuries of neglect to our own great period of musical achievements. The time will come soon when foreign musicians will discover that England once produced a great composer, and his influence will spread to a wider field. As a man he is the greatest in English musical history till Sir Hubert Parry, who resembles him in having been that particularly likeable person—the man who combines stability with sensitiveness, a thoroughly English character with an artistic temperament.

APPENDIX

THIS appendix contains the names of all of Byrd's compositions mentioned in the text, classified under their respective headings, with the number of the page on which they are discussed, with the name of the publisher and, in the case of sheet music, the price of the modern reprint. It also contains the names of pieces not mentioned in the text which are obtainable in modern publications.

T.C.M. = Tudor Church Music, the Carnegie edition, published by the Oxford University Press at 30s. per volume

O.U.P. = Oxford University Press, octavo sheet

S. & B. = Stainer and Bell. In reference to virginal music S. & B. signifies the fourteen pieces edited by Fuller-Maitland and Squire

H.M.V. = His Master's Voice series of gramophone records issued by the Gramophone Company

Fitz. = Fitzwilliam Virginal Book, edited by J. A. Fuller-Maitland and W. Barclay Squire, pub. 1899, Breitkopf & Hærtel. Copies are now difficult to obtain.

> N.B. There is a discrepancy of one between the references given here and the numbering of the 1899 edition owing to a difference in the method of classification.

Nev. = My Lady Nevell's Book, edited by Miss Hilda Andrews, pub. 1926, Curwen, £3 3s.

Fos. = Will Foster's Virginal Book, still in manuscript

Glyn = Miss M. H. Glyn's *Dances Grave and Gay*, pub. Winthrop Rogers, 2s. 6d., containing twelve pieces

Bantock = Bantock's edition of twelve pieces published by Novello, 4s.

Parthenia = Pub. 1611, and reprinted by The Musical Antiquarian Society in the 'forties of last century

Chester = Catholic Church Music series, published by J. & W. Chester, Ltd., in which are included eleven of Byrd's motets, edited by H. B. Collins.

APPENDIX

MADRIGALS ETC

All the madrigals of Byrd may be obtained from Stainer and Bell in Fellowes's *English Madrigal Series*, either separately for a few pence each, or in Vols. XIV, XV and XVI of the series which correspond to the 1588, 1589 and 1611 sets respectively, price 17s. 6d. a volume. A complete list of Byrd's madrigals may be found in Dr. Fellowes's *English Madrigal Composers*. The following list contains the madrigals and songs mentioned in the text, one or two separate publications, and a few comments on the gramophone records. In connection with the latter it is necessary to say that most of the records of Byrd's music were made at the time of the tercentenary in 1923, before the improved sound-box and electrical recording had been invented. Unfortunately there seems little chance of these records being replaced by new ones electrically recorded. So far only " This Day Christ was born " has been done.

Come to me, grief, forever. D.711.
Why do I use my paper, ink and pen? D.711.
The two madrigals are recorded on the same side of the disc. Like most of these vocal records this one does justice to the individual parts more than to the blend of voices. The bass is much improved on the new machine, but the high soprano of Miss Flora Mann still lacks a good deal of the solid tone which she possesses in real life.

APPENDIX

I joy not in no earthly bliss, Novello, 4d.
If that a Sinner's Sighs, 170
If gold all burnished, 178
If in thine heart, 179
If women could be fair and never fond, 176
In Fields Abroad, 168
Is Love a boy ? 175
La Virginella, 161
Love in a fit of pleasure, 180
Love would discharge, 177
Lullaby, my sweet little Baby, 170, 214. H.M.V. E.232

A desirable record and a clear one. The balance of voices, however, is
not perfect, the two top parts not being prominent enough. The second
soprano is described by Byrd as "the first singing part," i.e., it is to be
regarded as carrying the chief melodic line, yet in this record it is mostly
inaudible.

My little sweet darling (song), 170, 189. S. & B., 1s.
O God that guides the cheerful sun, 185
O Lord my God, let flesh and blood thy servant not subdue, 175
O Lord, who in Thy sacred tent ? 163
O you that hear this voice, 166
Penelope that longed for the sight, 177
Praise our Lord all ye Gentiles, 187. H.M.V. D.710

To get this characteristic work of Byrd's maturity is a matter for gratitude
and it is well and clearly recorded. It is difficult to follow with a score,
partly because the two extreme parts both in the treble and in the bass are
continually crossing, and partly because the singers are singing in a pitch
a minor third higher than the printed notes (at any rate of Vol. XVI of the
English Madrigal School), so that eye and ear are apt to mislead each other.

See those sweet eyes, 177
Sing we merrily unto God, 185
Sing ye to our Lord, 184
Susanna Fair, 174
The fair young virgin, 161
The Greedy Hawke, 175
The match that's made, 169
The nightingale so pleasant, 175

APPENDIX

This day Christ was born, 186. H.M.V. E.305 ; C.1334

E. 305

A good record in which the individual quality of each voice is easily distinguishable, so much so that the places where the English Singers have had (owing to the unusual scoring for voices which gives the madrigal its great brilliance) to change round among themselves, the inner parts may be detected by anyone following with a score.

C. 1334

The enormous improvement in the new recording upon the old may be seen by a comparison of these two records. It is necessary to bear in mind however, that the old record was made by a party of six soloists, the new by the choir of York Minster in their own building. There is no evaporation of bass tone to bewail in this record ; the whole is very massive and considering the natural echo of the building the words come through well. It may be noted that Dr. Bairstow disregards Dr. Fellowes's suggested marks of expression and tempo. " Hallelujah " is taken more slowly instead of more quickly than the preceding passages.

This sweet and merry month of May, 78, 183, 184. Six-part setting, H.M.V. E.292

This is a quick six-part madrigal, yet the parts are exceptionally clear. The new sound-box seems to have tilted the balance in favour of the lower voices, which formerly were unequal to the top parts. There is nothing to hurt, however, in this record, and the words come through well.

Though Amaryllis dance in green, 164, 188, 239. H.M.V. E.292

This is a good record of a good madrigal. The five voices retain their individual qualities and the ensemble is quite clear. The bass, even on the new machine, is still a little on the light side.

Turn our Captivity, 187. H.M.V. D.711

This is a 12-inch record of one of the big serious madrigals. The recording is clear so that the parts can be followed easily enough, but the quality of. tone is rather coarse.

What made thee Hob forsake the plow ? 179
What pleasure have great princes ? 169
While that the sun with his beams hot, 175, 176
Why do I use my paper, ink and pen ? 172 H.M.V. D.711

MASSES

Three-part Mass, 53. S. & B., 1s. 6d.
Kyrie, 54. H.M.V. E.290

249

APPENDIX

Sanctus, 54, 56. H.M.V. E.290

This is a good record on which to begin this sort of music. The part-writing is very clear, and gives a good idea of contrapuntal composition and the sort of beauties which it produces. The balance of the voices is well judged, though towards the end there is just a suggestion of effort which would probably be absent if a choir instead of a solo trio were performing the *Sanctus* with its continuous crescendo.

Gloria, 55
Benedictus, 55, 58
Agnus Dei, 55, 58, 60
Credo, 56
Osanna in Excelsis, 58, 62

Four-part Mass, 59. S. & B., 2s.
Agnus Dei, 59. H.M.V. E.290

In this movement the weaving of the parts gets gradually closer. The recording is clear, and the voices retain their individual qualities. The result is that a good idea can be obtained of the way in which the Elizabethan composers build up a mass of sound from the inter-weaving of well-defined single voice-parts.

Kyrie, 60
Benedictus, 62
Osanna, 62

Five-part Mass, 62. S. & B., 3s.
Sanctus, 62

MOTETS

Alleluia, Ave Maria, 73. T.C.M. VII
Angelus Domini descendit, 76. T.C.M. VII
Ave Maria, gratia plena. Chester, 4d.
Ave Verum Corpus, 71, 72, 74, 75, 240. H.M.V. E.305 ; O.U.P., 4d. T.C.M. VII

A quiet record ; a fair example of Byrd in his graver mood. The words are clearer than usual, and the balance of the voices is good, the bass in particular recording more firmly than sometimes happens. N.B. that there is a cut of fourteen bars before the " amen," which does not however matter very seriously as the part omitted is a repetition of what has just been sung. Musically the phrase " miserere mei " in imitation, and the elaborate plagal cadence which forms the " amen " call attention to themselves.

Beata es. Chester, 6d.

APPENDIX

Beata Viscera. Chester, 4d.
Benedicta et Venerabilis, 73. T.C.M. VII
Cantate Domino, 69. O.U.P., 4d.
Christus resurgens, 38, 75. Chester, 6d. T.C.M. VII
Civitas sancti tui [Bow Thine Ear], 65, 102. Chester, 6d.
Confirma hoc Deus. Chester, 4d.
Deo Gratias, 76, 238. T.C.M. VII
Dicant nunc Judæi, 75. *See* Christus resurgens
Dies Sanctificatus. S. & B., 3d. T.C.M. VII
Diliges Dominum, 51, 235.
Exsurge Domine, 68, 105. H.M.V. D.710 ; O.U.P., 8d.

A good example of Byrd in his most spacious and vigorous style. But it
needs repeated hearing because anyhow there is a lot going on and the blend
of the voices is none too good. The alto and the two tenors make a rather
confused noise in the middle, the soprano seems completely detached. But
it is a glorious piece of music which continually reveals new beauties. The
detail is in the record alright, and can soon be detected, while the general
sweep and urge of the work as a whole is immediately apparent. Two lovely
little points, both in the soprano part, add to the broad nobility of the whole
a touch of grace : (1) the little ornament on the word " nostrae " just before
the return to " exsurge " ; (2) the rise to the last note of all, which makes
the peak of the whole motet. The singers end half a tone sharper than they
began.

Hæc Dies, 69. 6 part setting, O.U.P., 6d. 5 part setting,
T.C.M. VII
Hodie Christus natus est, 78. S. & B., 4d. T.C.M. VII
Hodie Simon Petrus, 80. T.C.M. VII
In manus tuas commendo meum spiritum, 76. T.C.M. VII
In resurrexione, 66
Justorum Animæ, 74. Novello, 4d. ; S. & B., 3d. T.C.M. VII
Lætentur Cœli, 66. O.U.P., 6d.
Miserere mei, 69. O.U.P., 4d.
Ne irascaris [O Lord turn Thy wrath], 65, 102
Non vos relinquam orphanos, 79. T.C.M. VII
Non nobis Domine (3 part canon). Novello, 2d. ; Curwen, 2d.
O quam gloriosum, 66. O.U.P., 8d.
O quam suavis, 78. Chester, 6d. T.C.M. VII
O sacrum convivium. Chester, 4d.
Post Partum Virgo, 74. T.C.M. VII

APPENDIX

Psallite Domino, 79. T.C.M. VII
Responsum accepit Simeon, 73. T.C.M. VII
Rorate Cœli, 74. O.U.P., 6d. T.C.M. VII
Sacerdotes Domini, 75. O.U.P., 2d. T.C.M. VII
Salve Regina. Chester, 6d.
Senex puerum portabat. Chester, 3d.
Solve jubente Deo, 80. T.C.M. VII
Tu es pastor ovium. Chester, 6d.
Tu es Petrus, S. & B., 6d.
Turbarum Voces, 76. Novello, 6d. T.C.M. VII
Veni, Veni Sancte Spiritus, 79. T.C.M. VII
Victimæ Paschali, 79. O.U.P., 4d.. T.C.M. VII
Vigilate nescitis enim, 66, 67. O.U.P., 8d.

SERVICES

Byrd in D Minor, 87, 89. T.C.M. II
   Te Deum and Benedictus. O.U.P., 9d.
   Magnificat, 90. H.M.V. E.291 } Novello, 6d.
   Nunc Dimittis, 90   } O.U.P., 8d.

A clear record. There is a curious mistake near the beginning : the soprano sings a high F on the syllable *Sa* of Saviour instead of C, and three bars further on the same thing seems to happen again on the word "his" before "hand-maiden." In both cases the tenor has a high F and in the second case it might be a chance acoustical effect. The authoritative edition by Canon Fellowes gives no alternative reading for either place. In the first place the soprano leaves her high note immediately by dropping an octave on to her part as printed ; in the second she does a similar thing by dividing a minim C into two crochets C and F, and then returning to the B flat as printed. In this way no mistakes in the part-writing occur.

Second Service, 87. T.C.M. II
   Magnificat, 87   } O.U.P., 8d.
   Nunc Dimittis, 87   } O.U.P., 8d.

Third Service, 86. T.C.M. II
   Magnificat, 86, 87   } O.U.P., 8d.
   Nunc. Dimittis, 86, 87 } O.U.P., 8d.

Fourth Service in F., 88

APPENDIX

The Great Service, 88, 89, 91, 92, 93, 98, 240. T.C.M. II ;
   O.U.P., 6s.
   Venite, 93, 94
   Te Deum, 93, 94   ⎫
   Benedictus, 93, 94 ⎬ O.U.P., 1s. 9d.
   Kyrie, 93, 95
   Credo, 93, 95
   Magnificat, 93, 95   ⎫
   Nunc Dimittis, 93, 96 ⎬ O.U.P., 1s. 9d.
   Gloria, 96. H.M.V. E.291

No better short selection could have been chosen to represent the " Great "
Service than this *Gloria*, which brings a noble work to a noble end. The
voices have been re-arranged in performance and greater clarity has thereby
been obtained ; the second alto is taken by a tenor and the tenor is sung by
a baritone, since the part lies in the best part of a baritone's range. The
general effect is one of smoothness, sufficiently massive, but without thickness.

Preces Responses and Litany. T.C.M. II ; O.U.P., 8d.

VIRGINAL MUSIC

All in a garden green, 130. Fitz. 104 ; Nev. 32
Alman. *See under* Monsieur's and Queen's
Battle, The, 119. Nev. 3-5
Bagpipe and the drone, The, 121. Nev. 4
Barelye Breake, The, 123. Nev. 6
Bells, The, 135. Fitz. 69 ; H.M.V. C.1215
Buriing of the Dead, The, 122. Nev. 5
Carman's Whistle, The, 130, 131, 242. Fitz. 58 ; Nev. 34
Coranto. Fitz. 241 ; Glyn ; Fos. 19
Coranto, French, First, Second and Third. Fos. 2, 3 and 4 ;
   Fitz. 205 (second) ; S. & B.
Earle of Oxford's Marche, The, 119. H.M.V. E.294 ; Fitz. 259

This is perhaps the best of the harpsichord records. All the parts except
the extreme bass are equally audible. The brilliance both of the music and
of the instrument are fully realised. In two places Mrs. Woodhouse has
varied the pitch of a short passage by the use of a coupler.

Earle of Salisbury, The (Pavan), 136. Parthenia ; Bantock ;
   S. & B. ; Glyn.

Fantasia. S. & B.
Flute and the droome, The, 121. Nev. 4.
Fortune. Fitz. 65. Fos. 43. Breitkopf Selection.
French Corantos. *See above, under* Coranto
Galliard. Fitz. 255; H.M.V. E.295

The opening chords sound out of tune. Whether this is so or no, the F sharp is very subdued, and this enhances the modal effect. Where the couplers are drawn and the tone is massive a percussive effect almost like that of a piano is heard, but in the middle section the plucked tone is very faithfully reproduced.

Galliard following The Earl of Salisbury Pavan. Parthenia; S. & B.; Glyn
Galliards, Gygge A, 123. Nev. 7
Galliard, Sir John Grayes, 137. H.M.V. E.295; Fitz. 191; S. & B.; Bantock
Gipseis, Round, 132. Fitz. 216
Ground, Hugh Aston's. *See below*
Ground, The Second, 123. Nev. 30
Hugh Aston's Grownde, 132. Fitz. 60; Nev. 35
Huntes up, The, 124. Fitz. 59; Nev. 8
Irishe Marche, The (from The Battle), 120. Glyn
John come kisse me now. Fitz. 10. Breitkopf Selection.
Lachrymæ (*see under* Pavan), 137
Lavolta, 140. Fitz. 155, 159; Glyn
Lord Willoughby's Welcome Home, 130. H.M.V. E.295 (*See* Rowland)
Maydens Song, The, 129. Fitz. 126; Nev. 28
Marche of Footemen, The, 120. Nev. 4
Marche of Horsmen, The, 120. Nev. 4
Marche to the Fighte, The, 121. Nev. 4
Medley. Fitz. 172; Glyn
Miserere, 141. Fitz. 176; Bantock; S. & B.
Monsieurs Alman, 139. Fitz. 61; Fos. 42; S. & B.
Morris, The, 122. Nev. 5
O Mistress Myne, 134. Fitz. 66; Bantock
Pavan and Galliard, Earl of Salisbury (*see above*)
Pavana Fantasia, 137. Fitz.; S. & B.

APPENDIX

Pavan, from Foster, Glyn ; also S. & B., No. 14, entitled *Air*

Pavana, Lachrymæ, 137. Fitz. 121 ; Fos. 55

Pavan, Lady Monteagles. Fitz. 294 ; S. & B.

Pavane and Galliard, S. Wm. Petre, 136. Parthenia 2-3 ; Nev. 34, 40 ; Fos. 51-2

Pavan and Galliard, & Passamezzo, 124, 125. Fitz. 56-7 ; Nev. 24-5 ; Fos. 39-40

Pescodd Time, 124. Fitz. 276

Preludium, 141. Parthenia ; Bantock ; and another in Augener's selection

Queen's Alman, The, 139 ; H.M.V. E.294 ; Fitz. 171 ; Glyn

A brilliant piece, which benefits from the new soundbox. The diapason quality of the lower strings of a harpsichord is lost on a gramophone, but the evanescence of the treble register of the instrument is counteracted by the process of recording.

Qui Passe. Nev. 2

Retreat, The, 121. Nev. 5

Rowland, 130. H.M.V. E.295 ; Fitz. 160 ; Nev. 33 ; Fos. 6 ; Bantock ; S. & B.

A charming piece and quite a good record. The tone is not quite even, e.g. the treble of the first bar. Mrs. Woodhouse repeats the first two sections of tune.

Second Grownde, The, 123. *See* Ground

Sellinger's Rounde, 130, 131. Fitz. 64 ; Nev. 37

Sir John Grayes Galliarde. *See under* Galliard

S. Wm. Petre (Pavan *q.v.*), 136

Souldiers' Dance Ye, 122. (Nev. 4)

Souldier's Sommons, The, 120. Nev. 4

Treg. Grownde [Hugh Ashton's Ground, *q.v.*]   132

Trumpetts, The, 120. Nev. 4

Ut mi re, 142. Fitz. 102

Ut re mi fa sol la, 142. Fitz. 101 ; Nev. 9

Voluntarie, 123, 124. Nev. 24, 42

Walsingham, 130. Fitz. 65 ; Nev. 31 ; Fos. 12

Wolsey's Wild. Fitz. 157 ; H.M.V. C.1215 ; Bantock ; S. & B.

The military band records do not really give a fair idea of Byrd's virginal music.

255

APPENDIX

Woods so Wild, The, 129. Fitz. 67; Nev. 27; Fos. 17
Bantock

Miscellaneous

Canon. Non nobis Domine, 63. Novello, 2d.; Curwen, 2d.
Chant. When Israel out of Egypt came. S. & B. 3d.
Compline Hymn. Christe qui lux es et dies, 82. H.M.V. C.1334
  O.U.P., 4d.
Hymn. Preces Deo Fundamus, 193, 216
Solo for Voice and Strings. My little sweet darling, 170, 189.
  S. & B., 1s.
Strings. Four-part fantasia for strings, 1611, 146.
Five-part fantasia, The Leaves be green (Browning), 143, 145.
  Curwen. Score 3s. 6d., parts 1s.
Fantasia in six parts, 1611, 25, 143, 144, 145. H.M.V. E.293
  S. & B., score 1s., parts, 2s. 6d. extra parts 6d.

This is a lovely work which one is glad to be able to get for gramophone, but as a record it can only be described as bad. The four lower strings are almost inaudible and indistinguishable when the two violins are playing. Further, the violins themselves are liable to sudden weakness on high Gs and As. Passages in thirds and tenths (e.g. last section, letter G in the score) between two parts record unevenly. In fact the record is uneven from every point of view, yet it somehow manages to convey the pastoral atmosphere of the piece. The fantasia is divided at the end of the first of the three sections, and a chord of C is inserted as a point of repose while the record is turned. On the new gramophone the bass parts fare better, though the record is by no means perfect in the matter of balance.

Fantasia in six parts (Greensleeves), 143, 145. S. & B., score 1s.,
  parts 2s. 6d., extra parts 6d.
In Nomine, 25, 143

INDEX

257

INDEX

262

INDEX

INDEX

INDEX